UNIVERSAL LOVE

Lama Yeshe

UNIVERSAL LOVE

The Yoga Method of Buddha Maitreya

Edited by Nicholas Ribush

Lama Yeshe Wisdom Archive • Boston
www.LamaYeshe.com

A non-profit charitable organization for the benefit of all
sentient beings and an affiliate of the Foundation for the
Preservation of the Mahayana Tradition. www.fpmt.org

First published 2008

LAMA YESHE WISDOM ARCHIVE
PO Box 356 • WESTON, MA 02493, USA

Library of Congress Cataloging-in-Publication Data

Thubten Yeshe, 1935–1984.
  Universal love : the yoga method of Buddha Maitreya /
Lama Yeshe ; edited by Nicholas Ribush.
    p. cm.
  Includes bibliographical references.
  isbn 1-891868-19-5 (alk. paper)
    1. Maitreya (Buddhist deity) 2. Tantric Buddhism—Rituals.
I. Ribush, Nicholas. II. Title.
  BQ4690.M33T58 2008
  294.3'4436—dc22
                                        2007046545

10 9 8 7 6 5 4 3 2 1

Cover photograph of Lama Yeshe by Carol Royce-Wilder
Other cover pictures courtesy Maitreya Project
All other Lama Yeshe photos by Carol Royce-Wilder
Drawing of Maitreya in Tushita on page 49 by Lama Zopa Rinpoche
Designed by Gopa&Ted2 Inc.

Printed in the USA with environmental mindfulness on 50% PCW recycled paper.
The following resources have been saved: 38 trees, 1,761 lbs. of solid waste, 13,716
gallons of water, 3,304 lbs. of greenhouse gases and 26 million BTUs of energy.

Please contact the LAMA YESHE WISDOM ARCHIVE
for more copies of this and our free books

Contents

Publisher's Acknowledgments

WE ARE EXTREMELY GRATEFUL to our friends and supporters who have made it possible for the LAMA YESHE WISDOM ARCHIVE to both exist and function: to Lama Yeshe and Lama Zopa Rinpoche, whose kindness is impossible to repay; to Peter and Nicole Kedge and Venerable Ailsa Cameron for their initial work on the ARCHIVE; to Venerable Roger Kunsang, Lama Zopa's tireless assistant, for his kindness and consideration; and to our sustaining supporters: Barry & Connie Hershey, Joan Halsall, Roger & Claire Ash-Wheeler, Claire Atkins, Thubten Yeshe, Richard Gere, Doren & Mary Harper, Tom & Suzanne Castles, Lily Chang Wu and Hawk Furman.

We are also deeply grateful to all those who have become members of the ARCHIVE over the past few years. Details of our membership program may be found at the back of this book, and if you are not a member, please do consider joining up. Due to the kindness of those who have, we now have three editors working on our vast collection of teachings for the benefit of all. We have posted our list of individual and corporate members on our Web site, www.LamaYeshe.com. We also thank Henry & Catherine Lau and S. S. Lim for their help with our membership program in Singapore and Serina Yap for her help with our membership program in Malaysia. Thank you all so much for your foresight and kindness.

In particular, we thank Peter Kedge and the Maitreya Project for kindly commissioning and funding the preparation and publication of this book, and Doss McDavid for a generous donation that has allowed us to expand the originally planned volume with additional introductory material.

Furthermore, we would like to express our appreciation for the kindness and compassion of all those other generous benefactors who have contributed funds to our work since we began publishing free books. Thankfully, you are too numerous to mention individually in this book, but we value highly each and every donation made to spreading the Dharma for the sake of the kind mother sentient beings and now pay tribute to you all on our Web site. Thank you so much.

Finally, I would like to thank the many kind people who have asked that their donations be kept anonymous; my wife, Wendy Cook, for her constant help and support; our dedicated office staff, Jennifer Barlow and Sonal Shastri; Ven. Ailsa Cameron for her decades of meticulous editing; Ven. Thubten Labdron (Trisha Donnelly) for her help with archiving and editing; Ven. Bob Alcorn for his incredible work on our Lama Yeshe DVDs; David Zinn for his digital imaging expertise; Veronica Kaczmarowski and Evelyn Williams, FPMT Australia & Mandala Books (Brisbane), for much appreciated assistance with our distribution in Australia; Dennis Heslop, Philip Bradley, Mike Gilmore and our other friends at Wisdom Books (London) for their great help with our distribution in Europe; our volunteer transcribers; and Greg Sneddon, Dr. Su Hung and Anne Pottage in Australia and Jonathan Steyn in London for their help with our audio work.

If you, dear reader, would like to join this noble group of open-hearted altruists by contributing to the production of more books by Lama Yeshe or Lama Zopa Rinpoche or to any other aspect of the Lama Yeshe Wisdom Archive's work, please contact us to find out how.

—*Dr. Nicholas Ribush*

Through the merit of having contributed to the spread of the Buddha's teachings for the sake of all sentient beings, may our benefactors and their families and friends have long and healthy lives, all happiness, and may all their Dharma wishes be instantly fulfilled.

Editor's Introduction

WE ARE DELIGHTED to add to our collection of Lama Yeshe books and Wisdom Publications' series of Lama Yeshe's tantric commentaries[1] by publishing Lama Yeshe's teachings on the yoga method of Maitreya, which he taught at Maitreya Institute, Holland,[2] in 1981.

Buddha Maitreya was very dear to Lama Yeshe's heart. As well as giving this commentary on the yoga method Lama also taught two of Maitreya's five famous texts: *Dharmadharmatavibhanga* (*Discrimination of Phenomena and the Nature of Phenomena*) and *Madhyantavibhanga* (*Discrimination of the Middle Way and the Extremes*).[3] And of course, Lama initiated the Maitreya Project, the building in India of a five-hundred-foot statue of Maitreya, more information about which can be found at the back of this book.

Thus we were delighted when the Maitreya Project commissioned us to publish this book. When we had finished the first draft we realized that publishing Lama's commentary alone would make the book relatively inaccessible to people unfamiliar with tantra, so we decided to add some introductory lectures from Lama's 1975 teachings in the USA. Now the book has something for everybody and better introduces the general reader to Lama's unique teachings on tantra.

However, as Lama has taken pains to point out before: "...a word of caution to the intellectual. Reading tantric teachings on your own, without the power of the appropriate initiation, is just an intellectual pastime—only by practicing correctly, under the guidance of a fully

---

[1] *Introduction to Tantra, Becoming Vajrasattva, Bliss of Inner Fire* and *Becoming the Compassion Buddha.*
[2] An FPMT center in Holland, see www.maitreya.nl
[3] See footnote 12, page 46, for the names of all five texts.

qualified and experienced teacher, can you evolve beyond the intellect, beyond conceptual thought into the true wisdom of a pure, spontaneous being. I am not trying to be mysterious or exclusive here but simply saying that if you think that you can understand, let alone experience, the methods of tantric yoga merely by reading books, you are deceiving yourself—like a terminally ill person doctoring himself with the same methods that made him ill in the first place."[4]

In other words, simply reading books about tantra does not qualify us to practice it. For that, we need initiation and qualified guidance. So the question then arises, why publish books on tantra? It's true that in times past such teachings were secret and not made available to non-initiates. Things today are different. So many books on tantra are being published by so many unqualified authors that no less an authority than His Holiness the Dalai Lama has said that teachings that once would have been kept secret should now be published in order to correct mistakes made by inauthentic writers.

That said, Lama does tell the Maitreya students, "In the future, in my absence or that of another teacher, I think it would be good for Maitreya Institute to organize retreats on this yoga method. Personally, I also think it would be all right for people who have not had the initiation to join such retreats. Because this is Maitreya Institute we can make the exception that people can practice Maitreya without initiation. There would be many benefits from that. In Tibet we also had a system where people without initiation could join a group deity yoga retreat but could not do the practice individually."[5]

So, thanking Wendy Cook and Jennifer Barlow for their kind and helpful editorial suggestions, I hope you enjoy Lama's teachings in this book and are inspired to go deeply into the practice, find a fully qualified teacher like Lama himself, and quickly reach your ultimate mental and spiritual potential, enlightenment, for the benefit of all beings.

---

[4] From Prologue: Intellectuals, Beware! *Becoming Vajrasattva*, page 5.
[5] See page 102.

PART 1

Introduction to Buddhism

1. What is Buddhism?

I⟶'s DIFFICULT TO SAY "Buddhism is *this*, therefore it should be like *that*" or to summarize it in a simplistic way because people have a wide variety of views of what Buddhism is. However, I can say that Buddhism is not what most people consider to be a religion.

First of all, when we study Buddhism we're studying ourselves—the nature of our body, speech and mind—the main emphasis being on the nature of our mind and how it works in everyday life. The main topic is not something else, like what is Buddha, what is the nature of God or things like that.

Why is it so important to know the nature of our own mind? It's because we all want happiness, enjoyment, peace and satisfaction and these experiences do not come from ice cream but from wisdom and the mind. Therefore we have to understand what the mind is and how it works.

One thing about Buddhism is that it's very simple and practical in that it explains logically how satisfaction comes from the mind and not from some kind of supernatural being in whom we have to believe.

I understand that this idea can be difficult to accept because in the West, from the moment you're born, there's extreme emphasis on the belief that the source of happiness resides outside of yourself in external objects. Therefore your sense perception and consciousness have an almost fanatical orientation toward the sense world and you come to value external objects above all else, even your life. This extreme view that over-values material things is a misconception, the result of unreasonable, illogical thought.

Therefore, if you want true peace, happiness and joy, you need to realize that happiness and satisfaction come from within you and stop searching so obsessively outside. You can never find real happiness out there. Whoever has?

From the moment they evolved, humans have never found true happiness in the external world, even though modern scientific technology seems to think that that's where the solution to human happiness lies. That's a totally wrong conception. Of course, technology is necessary and good, but it has to be used skillfully. Religion is not against technology nor is external development contrary to the practice of religion, even though we do find religious extremists who oppose material development and scientific advancement and non-believers pitted against those who believe. All such fanatics are wrong.

First, however, let me ask a question. Where in the world can we find somebody who doesn't believe? Who among us is a true non-believer? In asking this I'm not necessarily referring to conceptual belief. The person who says "I don't believe" thinks he's intellectually superior but all you have to do to puncture his pride is ask a couple of simple questions: "What do you like? What don't you like?" He'll come up with a hundred likes and dislikes. "Why do you like those things? Why don't you like the others?" Questions like those immediately expose all of us to be believers.

Anyway, to live in harmony we have to balance external and internal development; failure to do so simply leads to mental conflict and restless states of mind.

So Buddhism finds no contradiction in advocating external scientific and inner mental development; both are correct but, depending on mental attitude, each can be positive or negative as well. There's no such thing as absolute, eternally existent, total positivity or absolute, eternally existent, total negativity. Positive and negative actions are defined mainly by the motivation that gives rise to them not by the actions themselves.

Therefore it's very important to avoid extreme views; extreme emotional attachment to sense objects—"This is good; this makes me happy"—only leads to mental illness. What we need to learn instead is how to remain in the middle, between the extremes of exaggeration and underestimation.

That doesn't mean giving everything up. You don't have to get rid of all your possessions. It's extreme emotional attachment to *any* object—external *or* internal—that makes you mentally ill; that's what you have to abandon. Western medicine has few answers to that kind of sickness. There's nothing you can take; it's very hard to cure. Psychologists, psychiatrists, therapists…I doubt that they can solve the problems of attachment. Most of you have probably experienced that. Attachment and the lack of knowledge-wisdom that underlies it are the actual problem.

The reason that Western health professionals can't treat attachment effectively is that they don't know how to investigate the reality of the mind. The function of attachment is to bring frustration and misery. We all know this; it's not that difficult to grasp—in fact, it's rather simple. But Buddhism has a method of revealing the psychology of attachment and how it works in everyday life. That method is meditation.

Excessive concern for your own comfort and pleasure driven by the exaggerations of attachment automatically leads to feelings of hatred for others. These two incompatible feelings—attachment and hatred—naturally clash in your mind. From the Buddhist point of view, a mind in this kind of conflict is sick and unbalanced.

Going to church or temple once a week is not enough to deal with this—you have to examine your mind all day long every day and maintain constant awareness of the way you speak and act. We usually hurt others unconsciously. In order to observe the actions of our unconscious mind we need to develop powerful wisdom energy, but that's easier said than done; it takes work to be constantly aware of what's going on in the mind.

Most religious and non-religious people agree that loving kindness for others is important. How do we develop loving kindness? First we have to understand how and why others suffer, what the best kind of happiness for them to have is, and how they can get it. That's what we have to investigate. But our emotions get the better of us. We project our attachments onto others. We think that others like the same things we do, that people's main problems are hunger and thirst and that food and water are the solution. The human problem is not hunger and thirst; it's misconception and mental pollution.

Therefore it's very important that you make your mind clear. If you can, the ups and downs of the external world won't bother you; no matter what happens out there, your mind will remain peaceful and joyous. If you get too caught up in watching the up and down world you finish up going up and down yourself: "Oh, that's so good! Oh, that's so bad!" If the outer world is your only source of happiness, its natural fluctuations constantly disturb your peace of mind and you can never be happy, no matter how long you live. It's impossible.

But if you understand that the world is up and down by nature and expect things to fluctuate, you won't get upset when they do and as a result your mind will be balanced and peaceful. Whenever your mind is balanced and peaceful you have wisdom and control.

Perhaps you think, "Oh, control! Buddhism is all about control. Who wants control? That's a Himalayan trip, not a Western one." But in our experience, control is natural. When you have the wisdom that knows how the uncontrolled mind functions and where it comes from, control comes naturally.

All people have equal potential to control and develop their mind. There's no distinction according to race, color or nationality. Equally, all can experience mental peace and joy. Human ability is great—if you use it with wisdom, it's worthwhile; if you use it with ignorance and emotional attachment, you waste your life. Therefore, be careful. Lord Buddha's teaching strongly emphasizes understanding over the hallucinated fantasies of the ordinary mind. The emotional projections and hallucinations that arise from unrealistic perceptions are wrong conceptions and as long as your mind is polluted by wrong conceptions you will always be frustrated.

The clean clear mind is simultaneously joyful. That's simple to see. When your mind is under the control of extreme attachment on one side and extreme hatred on the other, you have to examine it to see why you grasp at happiness and why you hate. When you check your objects of attachment and hatred logically, you'll see that the fundamental reason for these contrary emotions is basically the same thing: emotional attachment projects a hallucinatory object; emotional hatred projects a hallucinatory object. And either way, you believe in the hallucination.

As I said before, it's not an intellectual, "Oh, yes, I believe." And by the way, just saying you believe in something doesn't actually mean you do. However, belief has deep roots in your subconscious and as long as you're under the influence of attachment, you're a believer. Belief doesn't necessarily have to be in something supernatural or beyond logic. There are many ways to believe.

From the standpoint of Buddhist psychology, in order to have love and compassion for all living beings you first have to develop equilibrium—a feeling that all beings are equal. This is not a radical sort of "I have a piece of candy; I need to cut it up and share it with everybody else" but rather something you have to work with in your mind. A mind out of balance is an unhealthy mind.

So equalizing sentient beings is not something we do externally; that's impossible. The equality advocated by Buddhists is completely different from that which the communists talk about; ours is the inner balance derived from training the mind.

When your mind is even and balanced you can generate loving kindness for all beings in the universe without discrimination. At the same time, emotional attachment automatically decreases. If you have the right method, it's not difficult; when right method and right wisdom come together, solving problems is easy.

But we humans suffer from a shortage of intensive knowledge-wisdom. We search for happiness where it doesn't exist; it's here, but we're looking over there. It's actually very simple. True peace, happiness and joy lie within you and if you meditate correctly and investigate the nature of your mind you can discover the everlasting happiness and joy within. They're always with you; they're mental energy, not external material energy, which always fizzles out. Mental energy coupled with right method and right wisdom is unlimited and always with you. That's incredible! And it explains why human beings are so powerful.

Materialists think that people are powerful because of the amazing buildings and so forth that they construct but all that actually comes from the human mind. Without the skill of the human mind there's no external supermarket. Therefore, instead of placing extreme value on regular supermarkets we should try to discover our own internal supermarket. That's much more useful and leads to a balanced, even mind.

As I mentioned before, it can sound as if Buddhism is telling you to renounce all your possessions because attachment is bad, but renunciation isn't a physical giving up. You go to the toilet every day but that doesn't mean you're attached to it—you're not attached to your toilet, are you? We should have the same attitude to all the material things we use—give them a reasonable value according to their usefulness for human existence, not an extreme one.

If a kid runs crazily over dangerous ground to get an apple, trips, falls and breaks his leg, we think he's foolish, exaggerating the value of the apple and putting his wellbeing at risk for the sake of achieving a tiny goal. But actually, we're the same. We exaggerate the beauty of objects of desire and generate extreme attachment toward them, which blinds us to our true potential. This is dangerous; we're just like the boy who risks his safety for an apple. By looking at objects with emotional attachment and chasing that hallucinated vision we definitely destroy our pure potential.

Human potential is great but we have to use our energy skillfully; we have to know how to put our lives in the right direction. This is extremely important.

Now, instead of just talking, let me try to answer any questions you might have.

Q. How can I make my mind aware so that I have equilibrium of mind and skillfulness of action?

Lama. The first thing you need to do is to recognize how your unbalanced mind works—how it arises, what causes it to do so, what it reacts to and so forth—and how your false conceptions create the view you perceive. This recognition allows you to put your mind into a clearer atmosphere. Once you understand your unbalanced mind, it becomes clear.

The Buddhist approach to negativity is not to avoid it but to confront it head-on and check why it's there, what its reality is and so forth. We think that this is the best foundation for destroying the negative mind and is much more logical and scientific than just avoiding it—like running away to some other place or trying to think only positive things.

That's not enough. So, when problems arise, instead of turning away stare them right in the face. That's very useful; that's the Buddhist way.

If you run from problems you can never really ascertain their root. Putting your head in the sand doesn't help. You have to determine where the problem comes from and how it arises. The way to discover the clean clear mind is to understand the nature of the unclear mind, especially its cause. If there's a thorn bush growing at your door, scratching you every time you go in or out, pruning it won't be enough to solve the problem once and for all—you have to pull it out by the root. Then it will never bother you again.

Q. You mentioned going beyond thought. Could you please talk about that experience?

Lama. It's possible. When you suddenly realize that the hallucinated self-imagination projected by your ego does not exist as it appears, you can be left with an automatic experience of emptiness, a vision of shunyata. But as long as your self-imagination—"I'm Thubten Yeshe, I'm this, I'm that, therefore I should have this, I should do that"—continues to run amok, it's impossible to go beyond thought. You need to investigate such thoughts with skillful, analytic knowledge-wisdom. Scrutinize your mind's self-imagination as interpreted by your ego: what am I? What is it? Is it form? Does it have color? No. Then what is it? The only conclusion you can eventually arrive at is that it does not exist anywhere, either externally or internally, and the vision that automatically accompanies that experience is one of emptiness; at that time you reach beyond thought. Before that, your mind was full of "I'm this, therefore I need a house; I'm that, therefore I need a car; I'm the other, therefore I need to go to the supermarket." All your "I'm that-this" comes from conflicted emotional thought that completely destroys your inner peace....

Q. So then you're beyond thought and there's the void, emptiness?

Lama. Yes, that's emptiness or, in Sanskrit terminology, shunyata. But emptiness does not mean nothingness. It refers to an absence of ego conceptualization—"I am Thubten Yeshe"—which is bigger than Los Angeles but a complete hallucination. When we realize that it's totally non-existent, that it's only projected by the mind, by the ego, the experience of shunyata suddenly arises; at that time there's an absence of thought.

Now, "no thought" does not mean that you become somehow unconscious. Many people think that that's what it means but that's dangerous. Reaching beyond thought means eliminating the usual conflict-producing, dualistic, "that-this" type of thought, not lapsing into unconsciousness.

Q. Does Buddhism have physical exercises similar to tai chi or yoga, to tone the body as well as the mind? Are there physical exercises that are a part of Buddhism?
Lama. Physical exercise is good but mental exercise is better; it's more powerful. Nevertheless, we do have certain exercises but they're mainly to facilitate sitting meditation. Sometimes we do retreat in a small room for months at a time; on such occasions we also do some physical yoga. However, we normally emphasize that, no matter what actions we engage in with our body, speech and mind, mental attitude is the most important thing. Buddhism always stresses the importance of understanding the nature of the mind.

Q. How do we get rid of mental pollution?
Lama. By realizing *how* the mind is polluted, where the pollution comes from and that it has a deep root. If you know that, you can get rid of it; if you don't, you can't. Thus Lord Buddha always emphasized understanding as the only path to liberation, that the only way to attain liberation is through understanding.

Q. If everything is so simple and God is so perfect, why did he create all the negativity and suffering we see in the world today?
Lama. Perhaps it's *you* who created all the bad things you say God did. Our own mind creates our own uncontrolled situation. All the suffering we see in the world today was not created by God but by the negative mind.

Q. How can I escape the cycle of death and rebirth?

Lama. By recognizing and destroying that which causes you to cycle. Basically, if you're free of emotional attachment there's no cycle of death and rebirth. Once you cut emotional attachment, the cause, there's no reason to ever again have to experience an uncontrolled situation, the result. The short answer: cut attachment.

Q. When I read Zen and other Eastern philosophies, they all seem to be saying the same thing.

Lama. Yes, if you examine the different religions more deeply with right understanding, you'll find the same qualities, but if you just check them superficially you're more likely to be judgmental: "This religion's good; that one's bad." That's a poor assessment. What you need to look at is the purpose of each religion—every religion has a purpose—and how that purpose can be realized in experience.

The question is, however, do followers of a given religion know how to put its ideas into action? This is often the problem. People might think a religion's ideas are good but they don't have the key of method; they don't know how to put those ideas into experience.

Q. Then are you saying that your way of putting ideas into action is better than the others?

Lama. No, I'm not saying that my way is the best and that the others are wrong. I'm saying that most of us lack that knowledge. For example, you might say, "I'm a Buddhist," but if you check how much you understand your religion, how much you act in accordance with its principles, perhaps even though you say, "I'm a Buddhist," you're not.

I'm not talking about any specific person; I'm talking about all of us. So the most important thing to know is the method: how to bring lofty ideas down to the practical level, into our life.

Q. Lama, do you have anything to say regarding the interpersonal problems married people face?

Lama. Yes, I certainly have something to say! The main thing is that the two married people don't understand each other and this lack of understanding leads to poor communication and problems. Also, many times young people get married for very superficial and temporal reasons: "I like the way he looks, I like the way she looks, let's get married." There's no examination of the other person's inner personality or how life together will be. Because we can't see another's inner beauty we judge them by the way they appear; because we lack knowledge-wisdom we don't understand our spouse's essential inner qualities. Then, when the relative world moves on and things don't work out as we planned, it is very easy to disrespect our partner. Of course, most relationships and marriages are ego-based and so it's no surprise that they often don't work out.

It's important, therefore, that a married couple bases their marriage on mental rather than physical communication and that the two people really try sincerely to understand and help each other. A marriage based on superficialities will nearly always break down. Small things: the husband says, "Put this here," his wife says, "No, I want it there," and a huge fight ensues...over nothing! It's so foolish. Put it here; put it there—what difference does it make? It's so narrow-minded, yet we break up over these foolish things.

Q. Some people in our culture say that Jesus is God. How do you see Jesus Christ?
Lama. I see Jesus as a holy man. If you understand beyond words what he taught, fantastic. But we don't even understand what he said literally. Even though holy Jesus told us that we should love everybody, we still choose one atom to love and hate the rest. That's contrary to what he said. If you truly understand what Jesus taught, it's very useful, and especially helpful for mental sickness.

Q. Jesus also said, "I am the only way. Only through me can you reach God."
Lama. He did say that and that's right but you can't interpret it to mean that only his teachings are correct and that all other religions are wrong. That's not what he meant. "Only way" means that the only way to reach inner freedom is through the reality he taught. That's my interpretation,

anyway. Jesus saying "only my way" doesn't mean he was propounding some dogmatic view. He was talking about absolute reality as being the only way to God. If you realize that, you can reach inner freedom; if you follow your hallucinated, polluted, wrong-conception mind, you can't. That's how I interpret Jesus's words. I think that's perfect. Many people interpret what he said very dogmatically but that's just their polluted mind. So we have to be careful when we think we understand the views of other religions. Many times a religion's view might be perfect but our limited mind will think, "This means this, that means that," and all we're doing is bringing something profound down to our own mundane level.

Q. Is trying to plan and organize my life versus just letting things happen an expression of attachment?
Lama. Not necessarily. You can organize your life with wisdom. How? One way is by trying to make it beneficial to others rather than by living it simply for your own enjoyment. When your life is integrated and you're a wise, knowledgeable person giving a beautiful, peaceful vibration to others, it's so worthwhile. That's not attachment. Buddhism says that we can use our life and sense objects without attachment by giving them a reasonable value and using them to benefit humankind. We need both method and wisdom. You can eat ice cream without confusion or attachment; there's a way to transform worldly pleasures into the path to inner peace and joy.

Q. Can you talk a little bit about reincarnation?
Lama. Reincarnation is very simple; it's mental energy. Your physical energy is exhausted at the time of death and the energy of your consciousness separates from your body and goes into another form, that's all. That's the simple explanation. Mental energy and physical energy are different. Modern science has some difficulty with this. It does accept that there's a difference between mental and physical energy but Buddhism explains it more clearly.

2. The purpose of meditation

WE MEDITATE to experience how our mind works, not to change our ideas and philosophy or to try out some Eastern trip. We meditate to investigate the basic energy we already have, the energy of our body, speech and mind: what is it, where does it come from, why does it do what it does? This is not an external search; it's a search of our own mind and is so worthwhile.

Investigating our own inner nature, the reality of our own mind and life, is not just a religious undertaking. We can't deny that we possess body, speech and mind—we experience them all the time; we live within their energy field. So investigating our own energy to understand its true nature is really most worthwhile.

Furthermore, seeking the nature of the mind is not something that's necessary for young people but not the old; old people can't deny the existence of their own body, speech and mind either. Since the undisciplined, uncontrolled mind is common to both young and old, both need to investigate it. In fact, anybody whose mind is uncontrolled and produces agitation, conflict and frustration needs to look very carefully at what's going on. Such research is incredibly useful for young and old alike.

Investigating the mind doesn't demand an extreme change in habits, in the way we work, eat or sleep. However, the uncontrolled mind is intimately associated with the activities of our everyday life and causes the conflicts we experience all the time. Therefore it's essential that we understand the reality of our mind and the nature of our mental attitudes; this is most necessary.

The mind is like the central generator that provides electricity to the entirety of a big city; it's mental energy that determines whether the actions of our body, speech and mind are positive or negative, the cause of happiness or suffering. All the energy of our body, speech and mind comes from the mind. That's why Buddhism always stresses the importance of knowing its essential nature and how it produces both controlled and uncontrolled behavior.

How does Buddhism recommend we investigate the mind? The method is meditation. We receive teachings on the nature of the mind in general and on that basis experiment on our own mind; we investigate its nature through our own experience.

To our surprise, perhaps, we discover that meditation allows us to control small things that we could not control before. This encourages us to go further. We realize that far from being weak, we have fantastic abilities and potential. We stop thinking, "I'm hopeless, I can't do anything," and no longer rely on others to do everything for us. From the Buddhist point of view, the mind that relies on others is weak.

So what Buddhism is really trying to get us to do through philosophy, psychology and meditation is to become our own psychologist so that when problems arise we can diagnose and solve them for ourselves. This really is the essence of what the Buddha taught. Everything he taught was aimed at getting us to gain the knowledge-wisdom we need to understand our everyday life through knowing how our own mind functions.

Western psychologists also try to solve their patients' problems but not by making them their own psychologist. Patients who have mental problems need to realize the nature of their illness; then they can apply the right solution. If the actual cause of their problems remains hidden there's no way they can solve them. We have to realize the nature of our own problems.

Also, meditation doesn't mean sitting alone in some corner doing nothing; you can meditate while physically active. Your body can be moving but simultaneously you can be totally conscious and aware, observing how your mind communicates with the sense world, how it interprets the objects it perceives and so forth. That, too, is meditation.

Usually when we walk in the street, communicate with others, or do anything else we unconsciously leave imprints on our mind, imprints that will later ripen into problems. We call that karma. Most of the time we're unaware of what we're doing; that's the main problem. Meditation can wake us up and prevent us from sleeping our way through life. We think that when we're working, interacting with others and so forth we're awake, but at a certain level, we're still asleep. If you look below the surface, you'll see.

Thus you can see how worthwhile it is to understand the way your uncontrolled mind functions and discipline yourself with right wisdom, and to see that this is exactly what you need, no matter how old you are. With understanding, control comes easily and naturally.

The uncontrolled, undisciplined mind is, by nature, the opposite of knowledge-wisdom and happiness. Its nature is dissatisfaction. When you control your mind with wisdom you create the space you need to discover peace and joy. Your life then becomes peaceful and joyful and somewhat protected from the ups and downs of the external world. You enjoy life and stop blaming external factors when things go wrong: "I'm unhappy because society is up and down; I'm unhappy because of my circumstances."

Actually you have many reasons to be happy but your weak mind doesn't see that it's possible for you to be happy. Knowledge-wisdom is an antidote to the weak mind; it alleviates your depression and gives you the answer to all your problems. Knowledge-wisdom is the path to inner freedom, liberation and enlightenment.

Thus, through meditation you can discover how the selfish mind of attachment is the cause of all mental disease and frustration and how changing your attitude can make your mind healthy and give purpose and meaning to your life. The attitude you need to change is that of excessive worry and self-concern—"Maybe I'm going to get sick, maybe this, maybe that"—to one where through mind training you totally dedicate your life to the benefit of others. Attachment and self-concern are obsessed minds. The obsessed mind is automatically narrow. The narrow mind always leads to problems.

In the Mahayana teachings there's a mind we call *bodhicitta*, which means changing our attitude from obsessed concern for self-pleasure—"I'm hot, I'm cold, I'm this, I'm that"—to compassionate concern for other living beings' pleasure, and dedicating everything we do to the highest benefit of other sentient beings. That kind of attitude automatically brings relaxation and joy into our mind; everything we do becomes joyful and we see a much greater purpose to it.

Otherwise all we see are our imagined self's objects of obsession. When that's our view we very easily get unhappy and depressed. Depression and happiness don't come from outside but from how we direct our mind; not from changing our life but from changing our motivation. The motivation behind an action is much more important than the action itself.

With respect to actions, we can't say, "Doing this is totally bad; doing that is totally good." What determines whether an action is bad or good is our motivation for doing it.

Therefore we shouldn't ask others "How am I doing?" but look within to see what kind of mind impels our daily actions. Acting with attachment to our own happiness on the basis of an imaginary self always brings frustration and conflict into our mind whereas totally dedicating everything we do to the benefit of others automatically brings relaxation, joy and much energy into our mind.

Westerners over-emphasize physical action. For example, many people think that they're being religious when they give money to the poor or to worthy causes but often what they're doing is just an ego trip. Instead of their giving becoming an antidote to dissatisfaction and attachment it simply causes increased dissatisfaction and egocentricity and therefore has nothing to do with religion. Such people are just taking the religious idea that it's good to give and believe that they're giving, but from the Buddhist point of view charity is not what you give but why and how. True charity depends on motivation—giving without attachment or the expectation of anything in return. Such giving automatically frees the mind. Giving with the hope of getting something back is in the nature of conflict.

Therefore we have to carefully check our supposedly religious actions to make sure that they do in fact bring benefit and don't cause more confusion for others or ourselves. In order to make sure that our actions become positive, while doing them we meditate on the ultimate nature of reality or what's sometimes called the "circle of the three": subject, object and action. This is how to make whatever we do a true cause of freedom from suffering.

Investigating the nature of our mental attitude is most worthwhile, especially if we do it with the intention of changing attachment to the welfare of our imagined self into thoughts of benefiting others. In order to benefit others we don't necessarily have to do anything physical, we just have to turn our mind in that direction. This brings great joy into our mind, a warm feeling to our heart and clarifies the purpose of our life. We always think that the source of warm feelings is outside of ourselves but it can never be found out there. Warm feelings and satisfaction come from our own mind; that's where we should seek them.

Now I think I've said enough. Do you have any questions?

Q. You spoke of turning the mind around, changing the way we look at things. If I'm experiencing sadness or some other negative mind state that I don't like, how do I do that?

Lama. When there's a problem in your mind it's because of something you did in the past. For example, yesterday your friend might have said something that hurts your reputation and when you think about it today you get upset. That kind of problem is easily stopped. One thing is that your attachment clings very strongly to your reputation and worse, you *believe* that your being good or bad depends upon what others say. But the responsibility for being good or bad is actually yours. Somebody else's saying that you're good or bad doesn't make you good or bad. You're responsible. Also, whatever was said yesterday has already gone, so why worry about it? Anyway, this is just an example. You should know that whenever anything bothers you it's because of attachment, aversion or ignorance, a lack of intensive knowledge-wisdom, and that therefore there's a solution. There are antidotes to each of these three poisonous minds.

Q. Was tantra Shakyamuni Buddha's highest teaching?

Lama. Yes, definitely, but the main practitioners for whom he gave his tantric teachings were those who had the skill, intelligence and knowledge-wisdom to transform poison into medicine. If you don't have such wisdom, tantra can be dangerous, so please be careful. However, there's a way to develop your mind gradually so that eventually you'll be qualified to practice tantra; it's just not something you can jump into right away.

Q. I've seen Tibetan monks chanting. How does that affect the mind?
Lama. Chanting is a form of training in awareness of sense objects. Often our senses are totally unaware of what sense objects actually are. An object is there, our mind sees it, but then we project something extra onto it, something that's not actually there. Then we say, "That's good" or "That's bad." With chanting, our ordinary sense perception is transformed into blissful wisdom energy with total consciousness of the sense object, sound. So it's a form of mind training.

Q. It opens your consciousness more and more?
Lama. Yes, that's right. It allows you to see the reality of the sense objects you observe rather than the hallucinations projected by your ego. Actually, when you see monks doing puja and chanting, it might look like empty ritual but their external actions are just symbolic; internally, they're meditating. We all need to learn how to do that. Also, these practices usually come from the Buddhist tantric tradition. What's that? Normally, ordinary people might consider certain things to be negative, bad for their mind, but as I just mentioned, those with powerful, skillful, intelligent knowledge-wisdom and access to the methods of tantra can transform potentially negative things into positive. It's a kind of alchemy that turns poison into medicine.

Q. Would you say something about the role of women seeking enlightenment, please?
Lama. Men and women seeking enlightenment are the same. Women have the same potential for enlightenment as do men and equal ability to train their mind. The ability to develop powerful control over the mind and to reach enlightenment is equal. There's no way we can say that women are lower than men and can't do anything. Also, in Tibet there were many female lamas.

Q. What do you mean by control over the mind and how do we get it?
Lama. It comes through understanding the nature of the mind and practicing meditation. But control comes gradually, not all at once. You start off with a day's experience of control. When you find that as a result you're happier and more easy-going, you think, why not two days? Then a week, two weeks and so on. Developing control slowly-slowly is the way to go. You can't expect to gain lofty goals just by thinking about and grasping at them while you still have a low level of mind. It doesn't work that way. Progressing slowly and steadily is the way to reach spiritual goals.

The thing is, whether you're religious or not, it's important not simply to grasp at idealistic goals but to consider if what you want is achievable and by what means; ask yourself what you can do to achieve your aims. That is much more practical.

Sometimes we find that when things don't work out for them in the material world, people turn to philosophy or meditation but bring worldly grasping to their spiritual pursuits. Of course, that doesn't work either.

So I always get people to meditate in a step-by-step fashion. That's the comfortable way to proceed. You're sure of what you're doing, you gain experience and everything comes together for you in an integrated way.

Of course, we have many specific methods. Sometimes we use concentration on mantra and listening to our inner sound. However, in general, rather than getting involved in too much physical action, it's better to sit, relax and check your motivation. That's very powerful—much more powerful than watching TV.

Q. We're told to control our senses. Does that mean if I have a rose in my hand I mustn't smell it? What do you mean by changing or controlling our senses?
Lama. You don't have to throw the rose away to gain control; you can simply enjoy the scent of the rose in a reasonable way and not over-value it. For example, if you pick up a flower and think, "As long as I have this flower, my life has meaning. If I lose it, I'm dead," that's unreasonable; that's an exaggeration of the value of the flower based on a hallucinated view of it. The reasonable view would be to recognize that it's

impermanent; its nature is to come and go. When the time comes for it to disappear, you're OK with that. You're not fretting, "My flower is dead; my life is over." This shows how we create problems in our own mind. It's very interesting. Of course, we don't think consciously, "I like this. As long as I have it, life's worth living." But beyond words, deeply rooted within, we actually do have such a philosophy of life. There's a lot going on in our mind beneath the conscious level. That's what we need to check and observe through meditation. But getting back to the rose, you can smell and enjoy it; what you need to avoid is exaggerating its importance and getting attached to it.

Q. Lama, what's the best defense against worldly pain inflicted by other people when you're searching for wisdom and it makes you vulnerable to that pain? For example, if somebody tries to take financial advantage of you in business, should you fight back or be passive?

Lama. It depends on the situation. If you're well off and somebody cheats you out of a few dollars, instead of making a big fuss about it perhaps you can just let it go or even feel glad that he got some extra money. If it's a bigger amount, again it depends on how much it hurts you. One way you can assess the damage is to think how much longer you have to live. Of course, this is something we can never know, but say you give yourself five years—do you have enough for that? If so, then a few thousand dollars isn't going to make much difference. And you might not even live that long, so is a couple of thousand dollars worth hassling over? If you check, you'll see that you can never be sure how much longer you have to live.

Sometimes people forget what's of real value. They make millions of dollars—far more money than they could spend even if they lived a hundred years—and then finish up dying young, worried about the money they're leaving behind. If you're going to worry make sure you worry about something worthwhile. There are more important things than money.

Q. What I understand is that there are positive and negative worlds within us and we have to realize the positive rather than the negative.

Lama. What I'm saying is that we can make our mind positive, enjoy life and avoid putting ourselves into bad situations and conflict. That's the realistic way to live. We need to use the energy of our body, speech and mind to maintain what meets our human need, be content and avoid chasing excess. The "I need this, I need that" mind has no limit.

Q. Is bodhicitta the most beautiful or important aspect of Buddhism?
Lama. Yes, you could say that. Those who have realized the meditation on bodhicitta see all living beings as equal in the sense that none appear as close objects of attachment or distant objects of hatred. They have an equal feeling toward all beings—human, animal, insect, whatever. It's very important to train our mind in this.

Normally we always choose one person—which is like choosing one out of all the atoms in the universe—and cling to him or her, "Oh, you're my best friend, I can't live without you," with great attachment, over-estimation and grasping. When you grasp at one atom in this extreme manner you automatically discriminate other atoms as objects of hatred or indifference. This kind of unbalanced mind inevitably brings conflict and frustration.

So, in order to develop universal love and compassion, you need to feel equanimity with all living beings. This makes your mind very healthy. Lord Buddha himself said that you should not be attached to anything, not even the realization of enlightenment. If you are, then when somebody says there's no such thing as enlightenment, you freak out. That's *your* problem.

Often when you're attracted to a certain religion or spiritual philosophy you immediately exaggerate its good qualities and grasp at it, thinking, "Oh, this is fantastic; this is so good...." This can be very dangerous, because when somebody says that your religion's no good, you freak out. That's the unhealthy mind at work. Irrespective of the religion, philosophy, psychology or whatever else you follow, if somebody says it's no good and you get upset, that's *your* problem.

Therefore Lord Buddha said that we should not be attached to even the concept of higher realizations and enlightenment, let alone sense objects. He also said that we should not believe what he taught just because he taught it but scrutinize his words carefully with our own knowledge-wisdom to see if his teachings suit us or not. That responsibility is ours; we should not be Buddhists through blind belief.

Q. Could you please say more about the circle of the three, which you mentioned before?

Lama. I was saying that when we practice charity, for example, it's mostly in the mind; charity is wisdom. In Buddhism, charity doesn't mean just handing something over to somebody else. What often happens is that we hear that it's important to give but don't know how to do it correctly, so we make charity in the wrong way. Then, instead of becoming a solution to our attachment and dissatisfaction, our giving becomes just another source of conflict. We give and regret: "Oh, I shouldn't have given that away; now I need it." That's not charity. Perfect charity is made with the right motivation and awareness of the ultimate nature, or emptiness, of three things: you, the donor; the recipient of the gift; and the action of giving.

Q. Do you also have to check to see whether what you're giving is appropriate?

Lama. Yes, that's a good point too. For example, if you give money to somebody who then goes and gets drunk, instead of helping that person, you've given harm. That's just a simple example; there are many more.

Q. Would it then be charity *not* to give that person money?

Lama. Yes, that's right. Lord Buddha's charity is a psychological method of eradicating attachment and bringing the realization of inner peace. You can see how it works. If you give with an understanding of the ultimate reality of the object you're giving and the circle of the three—donor, recipient and action—there's no danger of a negative reaction. Our problem is that we always give with the expectation of getting something in return. Psychologically, that's a great problem. Therefore give with care.

Q. What do you think of the teachings of Christ?

Lama. His teachings were excellent. He taught what true love means, the shortcomings of selfishness and many other positive things. He meditated, too. Don't think that meditation is just an Eastern trip. By meditating on Christ's love we can transcend attachment and selfishness. He also emphasized forgetting oneself and focusing more on others' benefit. He was a great example to all of us.

Q. Did Jesus and the Buddha teach the same thing?
Lama. No, their teachings were different because they were teaching different people. Each person needs to be taught according to his or her own level of mind; the same teaching will not fit everybody. Therefore you can't state dogmatically that Jesus's teachings are all we need and that Lord Buddha's are unnecessary or that only Lord Buddha's teachings are correct and Jesus's are wrong. It all depends on the students' level of development—some who are not ready for one type of philosophy might be ready for another and only a skilled teacher can tell which is suitable for whom. Even within Buddhism, Lord Buddha taught thousands of different methods. You can't say that this one is right and the others are wrong, unnecessary. They're all necessary for certain people. That's why there are hundreds of different flavors of ice cream; people's minds are different. You can't say that vanilla is right and all the others are wrong.

Q. Does Buddhism not relate to an outside God, an outside savior?
Lama. Buddhism emphasizes that your main savior is yourself. Neither God nor Buddha is responsible for your positive and negative actions—you are. So you have to check your mind and motivation for doing an action *before* you engage in it; once it's finished it's too late.

Q. Is it possible to experience an inner teacher or guide?
Lama. Yes. If you're able to be intensively aware, you can get guidance or answers to your questions, but at the moment, how much of the day are you fully conscious and aware? An hour? Even less? So although you can make a little progress at times like that, most of the time you're unconscious. However, that leaves a lot of room for improvement. As you know, it's possible to be fully conscious day and night, so instead of

worrying, do what needs to be done to develop such awareness. If you can be fully aware and act correctly on the basis of wisdom, everything you do will be perfect.

Q. Then what is the role of an external teacher?
Lama. It depends on the individual. An external teacher may not be necessary. If you're already advanced through many previous lives' practice, perhaps you don't need an external teacher in this life. That's a question you have to ask yourself. If you have the inner wisdom to direct all your energy into the right channel, fine. But if you don't and always find yourself doubtful and hesitant, those are negative minds and should not be followed. In that case you need an experienced external guide. But of course, you have to check your potential guide's credentials very carefully before deciding to rely on his or her advice, and even analyze carefully check whatever you are told. If you think your own advice is better, then follow that. This is a path of personal responsibility.

3. Compassion and emptiness

THE MOST IMPORTANT THING those of us seeking enlightenment can do is to thoroughly analyze the actions of our body, speech and mind. What determines whether our actions are positive or negative, moral or immoral, is the motivation behind them, the mental attitude that impels us to act. It's mainly mental attitude that determines whether actions are positive or negative.

Sometimes we're confused as to what's positive and what's negative; we don't know what morality is or why we should follow it. Actually, it's very simple; we can check up scientifically. Moral actions are those that derive from a positive mental attitude; immoral actions are the opposite.

For example, when we talk about Hinayana and Mahayana it seems that the difference is philosophical or doctrinal, but when we examine it from the practical level we find that although literally *yana* means vehicle—something that takes you from where you are to where you want to go—here, this internal vehicle refers to mental attitude.

The practitioner who, having clearly understood the confused and suffering nature of samsara, seeks liberation from cyclic existence for himself rather than enlightenment for the benefit of all sentient beings has the mental attitude of self-concern and doesn't have time to look at other mother sentient beings' problems: "My problems are the greatest problem; I must free myself from them once and for all." That kind of mental attitude, seeking realization of nirvana for oneself alone, is called Hinayana.

In Mahayana, *maha* means great and, as above, *yana* means internal vehicle, so what makes this vehicle great? Once more, yana implies mental attitude and here we call it bodhicitta—the determination to escape from the control of self-attachment and obsession with the welfare of "I, I, I" and reach enlightenment for the sake of all sentient beings.[6]

We often say "I want enlightenment" but if we're not careful our spiritual view and practice can become almost materialistic. However, those who truly have the innermost enlightenment attitude of bodhicitta seek enlightenment *only* for the sake of others and thus become true Mahayanists. Those who seek self-realization out of concern for only their own samsaric problems are Hinayanists.

Why do we call these attitudes vehicles? A vehicle is something that transports you—in the case of the Hinayana, to liberation; in the case of the Mahayana, to enlightenment.

We talk a lot about Hinayana this, Mahayana that. We can explain verbally what these vehicles are, but actually, we have to understand them at a much deeper level. It can be that we're a person who talks about being a Mahayanist but is, in fact, a Hinayanist. What you are isn't determined by what you talk about but by your level of mind. That's the way to distinguish Mahayanists from those who aren't.

However, the way the lam-rim is set up is that it explains the whole path; it begins with the Hinayana and continues on through the Mahayana in order to gradually lead students all the way to enlightenment. It also demonstrates the step-by-step way practitioners have to proceed. The realistic way to practice is to follow the path as laid out in the lam-rim. You can't skip steps and jump ahead, thinking you're too intelligent for the early stages. Also, in order to experience heartfelt concern for the happiness of others instead of always putting yourself first, you have to start by understanding your own problems. This experience is gained in the beginning stages of the path.

There's a prayer[7] that says,

---

[6] In the *Tibetan Tradition of Mental Development*, Geshe Ngawang Dhargyey says (p. 202), "The Mahayana is called 'great' for the following reasons: 1. The aim is great, because it is for the benefit of all sentient beings. 2. The purpose is great, for it leads to the omniscient state. 3. The effort is great. 4. The ultimate goal is great, because it is buddhahood rather than mere freedom from samsara. 5. The concern is great, as it is for all sentient beings. 6. The enthusiasm is great, as the practice is not regarded as a hardship."

[7] In Lama Tsongkhapa's *Foundation of All Good Qualities*. See www.LamaYeshe.com.

Just as I have fallen into the sea of samsara,
So have all mother migratory beings.
Please bless me to see this, train in supreme bodhicitta
And bear the responsibility of freeing migratory beings.

It means that first we have to see that we ourselves are drowning in the ocean of samsaric suffering; only then can we truly appreciate the situation others are in. Then, by seeing that, we should not only wish to relieve them of their suffering but also take personal responsibility for their liberation and enlightenment; we must generate the determination to lead all sentient beings to enlightenment by ourselves alone. This is the attitude that we call bodhicitta.

Actually, what is bodhicitta? It's what this verse explains. It's not a situation of becoming aware of your own suffering, seeing that others are also immersed in it and then generating some kind of emotional sorrow, "Oh, that's terrible; how can I possibly help them?" That's not bodhicitta.

It's true that we suffer from the problems of ego and attachment and that all sentient beings are in the same situation of confusion leading to samsaric problems. However, seeing that and getting emotionally upset—"Oh, poor sentient beings, but what can I do? I have no method"—is not bodhicitta.

If you get too emotionally worked up over sentient beings' suffering you can even go crazy. Instead of your insights bringing you wisdom they bring you more hallucination; you pump yourself up, "I'm completely confused and negative, the world is full of suffering, I have no reason for living. I might as well slash my wrists and end it all."

It's possible to have this kind of reaction to seeing universal suffering. If you're not careful you might feel that this distorted compassion is bodhicitta. That's a total misconception. Bodhicitta requires tremendous wisdom; it's not based on emotional sorrow. Bodhicitta is the enlightened attitude that begins with seeing that all sentient beings, including you, have the potential to attain enlightenment. Before, you might have felt, "Oh, what can I do to help all sentient beings? I have no method," but when you see the possibility of leading them to enlightenment, a door somehow opens in your mind and instead of feeling suffocated and emotionally bothered, you feel inspired. Therefore, in the verse I quoted, bodhicitta is described as supreme, perfect or magnificent.

So there are two things we need in order to develop bodhicitta. One is, as it says, "Just as I have fallen into the sea of samsara." First we have to investigate and understand our own samsaric nature. When we realize that all our wrong conceptions and suffering come from the ego, we can extend that experience to others: "So have all mother migratory beings." Then, when we see our own potential for enlightenment, we see that all sentient beings have the same potential and take personal responsibility for leading them to enlightenment by attaining it ourself. This intention is bodhicitta; when the two thoughts—attaining enlightenment and others' welfare—come together simultaneously in the one mind, that's bodhicitta.

Seeing the possibility of leading all mother sentient beings to enlightenment and taking personal responsibility for doing so is very important. It automatically releases attachment and at the same time your actions naturally benefit others without your having to think about it.

Many people think that bodhicitta is a dualistic mind and therefore somehow contradictory because the Buddha said that enlightened beings have completely released all dualistic minds; they can't understand why we would purposely cultivate a dualistic mind. Some people engage in this kind of philosophical debate.

However, a mind perceiving a dualistic view is not necessarily totally negative. For example, when we begin to understand the nature of samsara, impermanence, emptiness and so forth, without first cultivating a dualistic view of these topics it's impossible eventually to realize them beyond the dualistic view.

It's very hard to transcend duality. Sometimes you can be experiencing a kind of unity but still find it has a dualistic component. The dualistic view is very subtle. Even a tenth level bodhisattva who has gained complete understanding of emptiness still has a slight level of subtle dualistic view.

Also, conception and perception of dualistic view are two different things. You can demonstrate this for yourself by compressing one eyeball slightly and looking at a single light bulb: conceptually, you know for certain that there's only one light bulb there, but what you see is two. The difference between conception and perception of dualistic view is like that. Therefore, when you first experience the wisdom realizing emptiness, you have the right conception but you still perceive things dualistically.

The reason we have not reached enlightenment since beginningless time is because our relative mind has relentlessly perceived things in a mistaken, dualistic way. The only unenlightened mind that does not see things dualistically is that of the *arya* bodhisattva in meditative equipoise on emptiness. Everything else is dualistic.

We often feel that analytical meditation is too hard because we have to expend a lot of intellectual energy checking this, checking that, and conclude it would be better just to stop thinking altogether, to completely empty our mind. That's just ego. How can you stop thinking? Thought runs continuously, like an automatic watch. Whether you're asleep or under the influence of drugs, thought is always there. Your stomach can be empty but not your mind.

From the perspective of Tibetan lamas, everything that sentient beings' relative minds perceive is not in accordance with reality. So where does this idea of the mind being empty of intellectual thought come from?

The experience of emptiness is not an intellectual one. If it were, all you'd have to do to experience it would be to fabricate it intellectually, "Oh, this is emptiness, I'm here," and then you'd feel, "Wow, now I'm experiencing emptiness." But of course, that's simply a polluted, deluded, wrong conception mind. It really takes time to experience emptiness. Nevertheless, there are degrees of experience. But for beginners, it's impossible to experience emptiness intellectually; it's beyond the intellect.

As spiritual seekers we face two dangerous extremes. One is over-emotionality: "I'm suffering, others are suffering, oh, it's too much, God help us!" Seeing everything as terrible is too emotional. The other extreme is over-rejectionism: "Nothing exists." You can't reject the reality of your own suffering...but through skillful wisdom and practice you can free yourself from it.

What we need to do is follow a middle path between the extremes of seeing everything with too much ignorant emotion as suffering and too much intellectualization as non-existent. But that middle path is very difficult to take.

Therefore Lama Tsongkhapa always advocated the simultaneous development of method and wisdom in order to realize enlightenment and negotiate the two extremes: that of no wisdom and emotional spiritual misery and that of over-emphasis on emptiness and rejection of morality and so forth. Method and wisdom have to be developed simultaneously.

Method means bodhicitta. And not just the words, "Bodhicitta is wonderful!" We have to practice it the way the lam-rim explains. If you don't have a perfect method for developing bodhicitta it will simply remain in your mind as a good idea. Therefore, if you do have a way of developing bodhicitta, you are extremely fortunate. Shantideva and Chandrakirti both explained how to practice bodhicitta, and based on their teachings Lama Tsongkhapa elaborated on how to actualize it in his.

One of the methods especially emphasized by Shantideva was that of equalizing and exchanging self and others [Tib: *dag-shen nyam-je*]: changing attachment to one's own happiness to attachment to the happiness of others. For countless lives we have always been obsessed with our own pleasure and have completely neglected that of others. This beginningless focus on our own happiness to the exclusion of that of others is called "self-cherishing." So we have to totally change this attitude to one of greater concern for others' welfare than our own.

Actually, this thought is extremely powerful; just generating it automatically destroys the ego. For example, if somebody asks us to serve tea to a visitor, resentment immediately arises within us. We serve the tea, but unhappily. As soon as we're asked, the buzz of irritation starts in our heart. It's amazing: we can't even be happy to give somebody a cup of tea.

The person who changes attachment to self to attachment to others doesn't have that buzz of irritation in his heart. Without even having to think about it, he's automatically happy to serve others. Psychologically, that's very helpful—it stops the pain of self-attachment from arising in our heart.

At the start of our practice, we beginners need tremendous understanding and strong intellectual determination because for countless lives we've instinctively thought, "My pleasure is the most important pleasure there is." Every minute, every second, that thought is there, even if it's not at the intellectual level. Attachment goes way beyond the intellect and is very well developed in our mind.

In order to destroy the instinctive experiences of attachment and self-cherishing we need to be strongly dedicated to the happiness of others; we do it not through the use of artificial force but by realizing that even the pain of losing our best friend comes from attachment. Nevertheless, even if this best friend asks us for a cup of tea, the buzz of self-attachment can still stir in our heart. It's incredible.

So we have to think, "Attachment has been a problem in all my beginningless lifetimes and it's still my real enemy. If I had to name my worst enemy, attachment would be it, because it hurts me all the time and destroys all my pleasure. For countless lives I have been concerned with just my own pleasure, which only results in misery. I must change my attitude from concern for my own pleasure to that of other mother sentient beings. Guru Shakyamuni Buddha attained enlightenment through concern for other mother sentient beings and helping them but because I've been on the attachment trip since beginningless time, I'm still totally confused."

Those who really want to realize enlightenment have to forget their own pleasure and completely devote themselves to that of others. That's the most important thing. It's actually a matter of psychology. At first glance you might think that this is just intellectual thought but if you really sincerely concern yourself with others' pleasure and forget your own, automatically your selfish motivation is released and you have less anger. That's because anger and hatred come from the selfish motivation that is concerned with only one's own pleasure. Don't think about this from simply the philosophical standpoint; check up through your own everyday experience.

For that reason, Nagarjuna said, "All positive, moral actions come from concern for others' pleasure. Everything immoral and negative comes from selfish attachment."

So that's clear, isn't it? We don't just make this stuff up philosophically.

It's scientific experience. Check your everyday life: ever since you were born you've been dealing with other human beings. You can't live without involvement with other people; it's impossible—unless you become Milarepa. But even if you do, you won't be Milarepa forever.

So bodhicitta is very practical. You don't have to intellectualize too much. Just check up every day how the self-cherishing thought agitates your mind. Even if somebody asks you for a cup of tea you get irritated. That's unbelievable, but it's your ego. So you bring the person a cup of tea and begrudgingly dump it down, "Here's your tea," but even though you brought the person some tea, because you did it with selfishness buzzing in your heart, it's negative. On the other hand, if you give somebody a cup of tea with the dedicated thought of bodhicitta, it's the most positive thing you can do: all the wonderful qualities of the omniscient enlightened mind come from concern for other beings' pleasure.

Just having this understanding is very powerful. For a start—forget about enlightenment—it makes your everyday life happy; you have no problems with those around you. It's extremely practical. Therefore, as much as you can, train your mind in bodhicitta and try to realize that attachment is the greatest obstacle to the happiness of your daily life. And even if you can't completely change attachment to your own pleasure to concern for that of others, at least you can try to practice the equilibrium meditation,[8] which is also a very powerful and practical way of bringing enjoyment into your life.

Perhaps, instead of arrogantly going for the realization of enlightenment, you can first try to make your daily life joyful by putting a stop to the things that come from the selfish thought and complicate everything. For beginners, this is probably more realistic and sensible. Just look at your everyday life and see how selfish attachment causes all the problems that arise.

All the problems of desire come from attachment; all those due to hatred and anger also come from attachment. Even a bad reputation or the upset that arises when you're insulted come from attachment. If you

[8] See the Appendix in Lama Yeshe's *Ego, Attachment and Liberation* (a free book from the Lama Yeshe Wisdom Archive).

really understand this evolution you'll have fewer problems and be psychologically healthy because understanding allows you to release emotional attachment so that it no longer has a hold on you.

What I'm saying is that sometimes we intellectualize too much about the highest goal—enlightenment—and neglect to investigate how our everyday problems arise. This only throws our life into disorder and is not a practical approach.

What's practical is to check how everyday problems arise. That's the most important thing and that's what practicing Dharma means. By constantly checking what kind of mind causes our problems, we're always learning. By understanding the nature of attachment we can easily recognize it when it arises. If you don't know how to look, you'll never see.

I don't need to say much more now but if you have any questions I'll try to answer them.

Q. Say we have the Mahayana thought and want to bring pleasure to others. There are so many of them—how do we decide who to help and how?

Lama. When I say that we should be more concerned for others' pleasure than our own, I don't mean that you literally have to help *all* beings right *now*. Of course, that's impossible—that's the point we have to understand. When you generate the wish to help infinite other beings and then look more deeply into what's involved in doing so, you'll see that at the moment, your mind, wisdom and actions are too limited to help all living beings and that in order to do so you'll need to develop the infinite, transcendental knowledge-wisdom of a buddha. When you become a buddha you can manifest in billions of different aspects in order to reach and communicate with all the different sentient beings in their own language according to their level of mind. So, understanding that you can't do this now but that you do have the potential to reach enlightenment and then *really* help them, you start to practice your yana until it eventually carries you all the way to buddhahood, when you can be of true benefit to others. However, this doesn't mean you can't be of some help to others now, even though it's limited.

The path to enlightenment has three main levels. The first leads us to upper rebirths but not out of cyclic existence; from here, the help we can give others is minimal. The second level is for those who seek complete liberation from cyclic existence mainly out of concern for their own problems. Even though such practitioners transcend their ego, the help they can give others is still quite limited; they can't help all mother sentient beings. Only fully enlightened beings can help all sentient beings—if that's what you want to do, that's the goal you have to reach, and that's where the third, or highest, level of the path leads.

Helping others has to be understood as rather more than, "I want to share my furniture with others" and then sawing it up into little pieces and distributing them evenly among your friends. That's not the way to help others. The emphasis has to be on training the mind. Otherwise it sounds a bit like communist propaganda: I have to share everything I own with everybody else. That's wrong; it's emotional. The communist idea of equality is false because it's not based on mind training. It's just another ego trip. It's impossible to achieve true equality just by saying, "Everybody should be equal," with ego, attachment and no mind training. You can't control people's minds with guns—from the outside it might look like control, but it's not.

The goal is to change self-attachment to concern for others. This is based on equilibrium, which is achieved through meditation, not physically. It's psychological, mind training, and very different from the communist idea of equality. Look at the Soviet Union, for example. Their original goal was equality but now they're becoming more and more like America. Why? Because they have attachment; everybody wants to be happy. It's the same with China. The cyclic nature of samsara is reality. The same things come around again and again. I'm not making some kind of telepathic prediction; you can see through logical analysis how it works.

Q. In thinking about the two vehicles, it seems that the Hinayana is quite strict in prohibiting certain actions—not killing, stealing, engaging in sexual misconduct and so forth—whereas the Mahayana says motivation is more important than action. Also, Nagarjuna quoted the Buddha as saying, out of his great compassion, that we should have few possessions and be content because it's very difficult for us to know our motivation. So it would seem to me that at our level we should follow the Hinayana, not the Mahayana.

Lama. I agree that it's better to have fewer possessions rather than to be surrounded by hundreds of objects of desire, pulling us this way and that and agitating our mind. However, Tibetan Buddhism puts Hinayana and Mahayana together; it unifies the two vehicles. Since our mind tends to run wild like a mad elephant, we definitely need to adhere to certain mental rules—following the disciplines suggested by experienced practitioners makes it unbelievably easier to practice sincerely and meditate properly.

For example, say you're at a busy airport with people rushing everywhere and I tell you, "Meditate! Meditate!" It's impossible, isn't it? Why? Because all your sense doors are wide open and you just can't focus your mind on one point. Similarly, if you sit down to meditate and I poke you with a needle, saying, "Concentrate! Concentrate!" you can't do it. Objects of sense gravitation attachment[9] are just like a needle—they automatically agitate your mind and by not avoiding them you make meditation difficult for yourself.

One lama said, "The more you possess the greater your superstition." It's true; the more possessions we have the more paranoid we are about protecting them and their constant presence in our mind causes it to be restless all the time.

In America, it's almost a right to possess a big house, a couple of cars, a refrigerator and all kinds of other stuff. Nobody looks at you twice and it doesn't necessarily take much effort to acquire such things. What takes effort is deciding, for example, what to have for breakfast; you have so many choices—"What should I eat? This? This? This? This? What about this?" It's such a waste of time; that kind of thing makes life difficult.

Take the middle path and choose your environment carefully; create your own mandala, just like Chenrezig creates his—surround yourself

---

[9] Editor: For several years I thought Lama was trying to say "sense *gratification* attachment" and would try to correct him (to no avail) but eventually it became clear that he knew what he was saying and meant the irresistible gravitational pull that objects of attachment have upon our mind.

with people and things conducive to your practice. Sometimes we're very weak; we think everything's so difficult. However, you have to know that human problems can be solved by human wisdom. So create your own mandala according to the way in which you want to develop—select carefully the kind of people with whom you want to associate, the kind of house in which you want to live, the activities in which you engage and so forth. That's very important. Otherwise you're just left with "Whatever happens happens. Who knows?" That's not the right approach. Karma is strong. Just because you want something to work out in a certain way doesn't mean it will go the way you want but if you put yourself into the right environment, you give yourself every opportunity to develop the way you'd like.

Q. Thinking about all this creates a bit of a dilemma for me. In a land of excess like America, it would seem that the fewer possessions I have the less my attachment and the greater my ability to think clearly and therefore benefit others. On the other hand, if I had a nice big house with lots of bedrooms perhaps I could help people more by giving them a good place to live, food to eat and the opportunity to meditate while being supported in this way.

Lama. If you have skillful wisdom it's definitely possible that you could help others like that, but if your mind is unclear and you make your offer emotionally, ten days later you're going to be saying, "The kitchen's a mess, there's a broken window, last night he did this, today she did that...." You get upset; others get upset—unfortunately, things can turn out like that. If you can execute your plan with wisdom and keep it all together skillfully, then of course helping others in the way you suggest would be a great thing to do, but first think it through and weigh your options carefully.

Getting back to the issue of mental rules, however, it's important to follow them at the outset of your practice but after some time, if you have skillful wisdom, perhaps you don't need them any more.

Q. I'm wondering how others and I should relate to you as a lama. Should we think of you as a person too?

Lama. Of course! I'm just another man.

Q. I mean, it's very hot outside today and although it's OK for me, I understand that it might be bad for you.[10] Since you're a lama, am I allowed to think in that way? Somebody told me that we should never think of a lama as an ordinary person.
Lama. Of course I'm a person. At the moment I'm manifesting as an American man from Wisconsin!

Q. Lama, where do you draw the line between putting yourself into situations—for instance, a job—where you have many opportunities to see your self-cherishing but where unconsciously you're also creating a lot of negative karma, and not putting yourself into situations where the negative mind can easily arise like this?
Lama. That depends. For example, if you don't put yourself into that kind of situation perhaps you won't have any money to sustain your life. Say you can't get a job other than one that will disturb your mind. You can take it and try to use that opportunity to understand your mental disturbances and in that way develop wisdom. It's a mixed situation, part negative and part positive. If you have little choice other than to take that job, then you've got to try to make the positives outweigh the negatives, but if you think that that is beyond your capabilities and will just lead to a nervous breakdown, then obviously it's better to try to find some other kind of work. You have to assess all this for yourself. However, if you're skillful, you'll try to find a Dharma job that offers peace and happiness and the opportunity to benefit others.

Q. My present job is driving a cab, so there are all sorts of people getting into the car all day long and I have many opportunities to practice the equilibrium meditation, but what I was asking was, is that type of situation good, where there's all this material to reflect on during my

[10] It was common knowledge among Lama's students that he had a heart condition that was aggravated by hot weather even though he never complained himself.

meditation at night but at the same time I'm creating a lot of negative karma during the day, getting angry, for example?

Lama. Again, it depends. If you assess the situation as basically more positive, then a little anger might be OK. Developing yourself for the benefit of others is better than a little anger. You can think, "My anger makes me go a bit crazy but as long as I'm helping others, I don't care." Giving yourself up for the sake of others automatically makes your craziness disappear.

Thank you. I think that's all the questions we have time for. We should now dedicate our merit. Dedication is very important. We often do positive things without dedicating the merit and as a result, as soon as we get angry that merit is destroyed. It's all about mental energy. So whenever you do something worthwhile, instead of puffing up with pride—"I did great"—or at some point getting angry, all of which dissipates your positive energy, sincerely dedicate your merit to others. This is an essential part of mind training. So beginning with bodhicitta, the determination to lead all mother sentient beings to enlightenment, do whatever action it is you're doing and then dedicate your merit: this helps make the action complete.

If we're not aware of these three—motivation, action and dedication—all our actions are incomplete and therefore not particularly powerful. On the other hand, when we do negative actions, even without thinking, we do them perfectly from beginning to end: we're motivated by strong desire, we do the action with great enthusiasm, and when we finish we think, "That was so good," sort of dedicating it to attachment. So from beginning to end it becomes a perfect negative action.

Mahayana practice is the complete antidote to perfect negative actions. At the beginning we generate bodhicitta, which completely neutralizes self-cherishing. Then we engage in a positive action. Finally, instead of feeling proud, we sincerely dedicate the merits of that to others. In that way it becomes totally positive.

Other religions may not be complete in the same way. They might start with good motivation but be bad in the middle, or the middle might be OK, but there's no dedication. Such incomplete practices can't be proper antidotes to attachment. If you look at the psychology of the Mahayana you'll see that the entire practice—motivation, action, dedication—is geared toward the destruction of attachment. You have to understand the psychology of your practice in order to know the purpose of what you're doing.

PART 2

The Yoga Method of Buddha Maitreya

4. A Brief History of Maitreya Buddha[11]

Countless eons ago, having made many offerings, Maitreya took bodhisattva vows from the *tathagata* Great Power in front of many other buddhas. From that moment on he has led countless sentient beings to enlightenment, guiding them along the path of the three higher trainings of discipline, concentration and wisdom by means of the three vehicles: Shravakayana, Pratyekabuddhayana and Mahayana.

While practicing as a bodhisattva he specialized in the meditation on great love. He not only taught this path to others but also meditated upon it continuously himself, often stationing himself at the gate of a city and contemplating deeply on loving kindness. His meditation was so powerful that people passing by close enough to touch his feet would themselves receive the realization of great love. This greatly pleased the tathagatas of the ten directions, who rejoiced in his actions and predicted that in all his future lives as a bodhisattva and a buddha he would be known as "Love" [Skt: Maitreya; Tib: Jampa]. This is how he received his name.

In one of those lifetimes Maitreya was born as one of the thousand sons of a great king. This king wanted to know in which order his sons would become enlightened, so he put all their names into a bowl, meditated deeply for seven days while performing many ritual offerings, and then drew the names out of the bowl one by one. Maitreya's name came out fifth, and the buddha of that age, the tathagata Limitless Knowledge, predicted that Maitreya would be the fifth buddha of the present era, Shakyamuni being the fourth.

---

[11] We're not sure where this prologue came from or who translated it from what, but it was published in the sadhana distributed by Maitreya Institute at the time Lama Yeshe gave this teaching in 1981.

Eventually Maitreya advanced through all the levels of spiritual development, achieved the tenth and highest level of a bodhisattva, and afterwards became a fully enlightened buddha. Having reached this level of utmost perfection, he manifested in many different aspects in countless buddha fields; at present his particular abode is the pure land of Tushita, where he imparts Mahayana teachings to countless advanced bodhisattva disciples. It was here that he taught his five famous texts[12] to the great Arya Asanga. Maitreya also gives many other teachings, in accordance with the needs of different disciples. He appears as countless spiritual masters throughout the ten directions of space, thereby leading innumerable beings along the path to full awakening.

Finally the time will come for Maitreya to appear as the fifth universal buddha of this world age and turn the wheel of Dharma for the benefit of all. This will come about in the following manner.

In the future, because of the growth of delusion, the beings in this world will degenerate—their lifespan will decrease and their lives will be filled with much suffering. When human life expectancy has decreased to only ten years, Maitreya will manifest in the form of a great spiritual leader and demonstrate the path of virtue. In particular, he will spread the teachings on loving kindness and, as a result, the fortune of the humans in this world will begin to improve—they will gradually give up their deluded attitudes and harmful behavior and their lifespan will start to increase. After many eons it will have grown enormously and people will live for 80,000 years. Then their lifespan will slowly decrease again until it reaches about one hundred. According to the prophesies of all the buddhas and his own promise, this is when Maitreya Buddha will appear in the world as a universal teacher, or founding buddha, like Shakyamuni.

His father will be King Great Compassionate Brahmin and his mother

---

[12] *Discrimination of Phenomena and the Nature of Phenomena* (*Dharmadharmatavibhanga*; *Chö-dang-chö-nyi-nam-par-che-pa*); *Discrimination of the Middle Way and the Extremes* (*Madhyantavibhanga*; *U-dang-tha-nam-par-che-pa*); *Ornament for the Mahayana Sutras* (*Mahayanasutralamkarakarika*; *Theg-pa-chen-po'i-do-de'i-gyän-gyi-tsig-le'ur-che-pa*); *Ornament for Clear Realization* (*Abhisamayalamkara*; *Ngon-par-tog-pa'i-gyän*); *Sublime Continuum of the Great Vehicle* (*Mahayanottaratantrashastra*; *Theg-pa-chen-po-gyü-la-ma'i-tän-chö*).

Queen Youthful-Looking One. Maitreya will be born from her side as she stands in a forest garden and the great celestial king Indra will receive the newborn buddha with great devotion. Immediately the baby Maitreya will take seven steps in each of the four cardinal directions and on each spot that he places his feet a treasure of lotuses will bloom. He will then declare, "I am the unsurpassed savior of the world and have come to liberate all beings from suffering. This will be my last rebirth; there will be no further reincarnations for me." Upon hearing this, all the exalted beings and spirits of the world will rejoice, perform many acts of purification and present him with magnificent offerings. His proud father will then take him around the city so that the citizens can also rejoice at their new treasure. Beautiful goddesses will offer him flowers and the great sages will predict that in that very life he will become a fully enlightened buddha.

Thereafter he will follow the life of a royal prince. When the time comes for him to be educated Maitreya will be the foremost of 4,080 students; when it is time to marry he will have many wives, with whom he will live for ten thousand years. Then a great religious festival of brahmins will take place in his kingdom, during which Maitreya will demonstrate that he has come to realize the impermanent nature of phenomena; seeing the example of the ascetic monks, he will declare his renunciation of cyclic existence and his intention to leave his royal surroundings and follow the religious way of life. This decision will so greatly shock those around him that the whole palace and all his wives will fly up into space.

Having made this decision to abandon the royal way of life, Maitreya will depart into the forest. All the celestial beings and saints will rejoice at his resolve, offer prayers for his success and protect and care for him as he meditates. Following his example, many of his wives, 1,040 members of his retinue and numerous city dwellers will follow after him in great devotion and also take ordination as religious practitioners.

For seven days Maitreya will follow the ascetic way of life, refraining from all food and drink. Then, upon arising from a state of deep meditative concentration, he will receive a bowl of milk from his wife Dawa'i Tongchen. Refreshed, he will assume the *vajra* crossed-legged posture and make the firm determination not to rise from meditation until he has achieved enlightenment. That evening he will defeat all demonic interferences and negative forces (Mara) and in the middle of the night will enter a state of profound meditative absorption. Finally, with the rising sun the following morning, Maitreya—who in fact achieved full enlightenment many eons before—will demonstrate for the sake of his fortunate disciples the attainment of complete and perfect buddhahood. Then, in the same manner as all the buddhas of the past, present and future, he will lead countless beings out of suffering and along the path to full spiritual awakening.

For seven weeks after his demonstration of enlightenment Maitreya will remain in silence, observing his future disciples. Then Indra, the king of the celestial beings, will present him with a golden wheel and the universally beautiful objects of the five senses and request him to turn the wheel of Dharma for the benefit of all. In response to this request Maitreya will teach the four noble truths, thereby leading many millions of disciples to liberation.

During his long teaching career Maitreya will turn the wheel of great teachings three times and each time countless multitudes of disciples will come to listen. These teachings will be enormous events attracting not only human, Earth-born disciples but also many celestial beings, *dakas, dakinis* and beings from other realms, many of whom will immediately become arhats, bodhisattvas and even fully enlightened buddhas. Through the power of his holy body, speech and mind Maitreya will lead and satisfy all those gathered according to their individual needs and capacities, giving Hinayana teachings to some and Mahayana to others. In this way he will lead countless disciples through the three vehicles to liberation and enlightenment.

Maitreya will remain for 60,000 years, providing direct spiritual guidance to his many disciples during his lifetime and, after he passes away, his teachings will last another 80,000 years, indirectly benefiting many more. Thus, through the power of his great, enlightened loving-kindness, Maitreya will provide limitless benefit to countless mother sentient beings.

In the absolute sense Maitreya is subject to neither death nor rebirth;

he is forever benefiting all mother sentient beings. Furthermore, he once declared, "Anybody keeping just one vow of moral discipline purely during the time of Shakyamuni Buddha's teachings will become my personal disciple when I appear and I shall liberate all such disciples," and he faithfully keeps this promise, his sworn oath and pledge.

Therefore, those of us fortunate enough to have met the teachings of Shakyamuni Buddha and maintained some level of pure discipline are guaranteed to make direct contact with Maitreya, become his disciple and quickly achieve enlightenment.

Lama Yeshe dedicated the merit of this translation as follows: "Because of this merit, may our life's energy be dedicated to the realization of Maitri-love, the actual nuclear weapon capable of destroying all external and internal enemies, just as Maitreya Buddha did, and may we reach the great state of equanimity, in which there are no neurotic friends, enemies or strangers."

5. The Practice of Tantra

THANK YOU for your interest in the practice of the yoga method of Buddha Maitreya. Before I explain the sadhana—the method of accomplishment—I'm going to give a general introduction to the practice of tantra so that you'll have a better idea of what it entails.

Tantra comes from the Buddha

The first thing I want to say is that Buddhist tantra definitely comes from Shakyamuni Buddha. Before his enlightenment, when he was a tenth-level bodhisattva, the buddhas of the ten directions stirred him from his deep meditative absorption and said, "You've attained the highest bodhisattva level, which is completely free from ego conflict, emotional problems and anxiety, but to discover the omniscient wisdom and eternal bliss of buddhahood, you have to receive tantric initiation." So they initiated him and he was then able to attain enlightenment.

One of the main tantric techniques enables us to handle pleasure in a positive way, to take pleasure as the path to enlightenment. A powerful king once said to Lord Buddha, "I'm confused as to how best to lead my life. I'm responsible for all the people in my kingdom and surrounded by worldly pleasure—what I need is a teaching to transform what's left of my life into the path to enlightenment." In response, Lord Buddha taught him tantra.[13]

For similar reasons I think that tantra is the right practice for Westerners and of the utmost need in this twentieth century. After all, the Buddha wanted us to have as much perfect pleasure as possible; he certainly

[13] See *Introduction to Tantra*, p. 13.

didn't want us to be miserable, confused or dissatisfied. Therefore we should understand that we meditate in order to gain profound pleasure, not to beat ourselves up or to experience pain. If entering the Buddhist path brings you nothing but fear and guilt then it's certainly not worth the effort.

The human problem

Our problem, our human situation, is that whenever we experience pleasure we get more confused; we react to pleasure by developing emotional confusion, hatred, anxiety and so forth. In other words, whenever we experience pleasure we lose control. Therefore Lord Buddha's teachings always emphasize gaining control of the mind.

So look within to see what happens when you experience pleasure: do you get more ignorant or less? Check that out—that's the main question. If whenever you experience worldly pleasure you become more mindful, concentrated, aware and in touch with reality, that's fine. However, it's more likely that you get further out of touch with reality, more spaced out, and enter an illusory, fantasy world of your own creation.

The two Mahayana vehicles

To help us deal with these issues, Lord Buddha taught two Mahayana vehicles—Paramitayana, or Sutrayana; and Vajrayana, or Tantrayana or Mantrayana.

So what's the difference between these vehicles? We already practice Paramitayana and the six perfections; we've all heard lam-rim teachings and are trying our best to actualize them—why do we need tantra?

The difference is that Paramitayana does not contain the skillful means for taking sense pleasure as the path to enlightenment, for transforming worldly pleasure into the path to enlightenment. This is the unique quality of tantra.

The difference is not that tantra offers us better or deeper explanations of shunyata, bodhicitta or renunciation. Those are the same in Paramitayana and Tantrayana. In fact, those three principal aspects of the path—

renunciation, bodhicitta and the wisdom realizing emptiness—are the fundamental prerequisites for entering the tantric vehicle.

Renunciation

Renunciation doesn't mean changing the color of our skin, putting on robes or not wearing make-up. Everybody, each human being, needs renunciation. Does that mean giving something up? Yes, it does—we all have to give up something—but what it is that we have to abandon is an individual decision; each of us has to check up for ourselves what extreme thoughts come into our mind and once we have determined what they are we should deal with them in an easy-going way. That's the way to renounce…deal with extreme emotions in an easy-going way.

I don't need to tell you the characteristics of your own emotional disturbances—you know from experience, "When I don't get this or that I get irritated." Thus you can figure out what you need to do in the way of self-correction to be happy. That's what I mean by easy-going with respect to renunciation. Anyway, I'm not going to tell you the details of renunciation, just its nuclear essence.[14] Each of us has to understand our own hypersensitivity and gross emotions, the problems they bring and the way to correct them. That's renunciation.

When Lama Je Tsongkhapa explained renunciation in his lam-rim teachings he went into great detail about ego conflict, its results and how and why people become dissatisfied, so you can research his extensive explanations for yourself.[15]

If you do, you will see that actually, renunciation is not that simple. From the Buddhist point of view it means learning about yourself by understanding how your ego works within your mind and how it manifests externally in your life situations and friendships. Therefore it takes a lot of wisdom. You don't just say, "Oh, I must renounce," and squeeze yourself. It doesn't work that way. Renunciation and meditation go together.

---

[14] See *Introduction to Tantra*, Chapter 5, for a more detailed discussion.
[15] See *The Great Treatise on the Stages of the Path to Enlightenment.*

Bodhicitta

Bodhicitta means opening your heart to others as much as you can. Normally we do open our heart to others to some extent—everybody does—but here we're talking about doing it with the highest destination in mind: the transcendent, universal aim of complete enlightenment. That's the way we create space in our heart. So it's very important.

We can see from our normal human relationships that when we're uptight and closed to each other it's extremely difficult to get along but when we open up and aim to achieve something more profound it's much easier. If I'm in a relationship with you only for chocolate, when I don't get my chocolate, I'm going to get upset, aren't I? From the Buddhist point of view, human beings are much more profound than that; we can achieve tremendous things. So bodhicitta is very important.

We think it's important to become a great meditator but that's very difficult to accomplish in this revolutionary modern world. These days it's much more practical to open our heart to each other and make that our Dharma path.

Still, it's a lot easier to say the words than to actually practice bodhicitta. Realizing bodhicitta is a process that requires continuous action and steady application rather than the occasional sporadic effort. The mind of bodhicitta no longer sees any objects of hatred or neurotic desire anywhere in the world and it obviously takes time to achieve the kind of equilibrium with all universal living beings that forms the basis of such a view. However, Buddhism is extremely practical and far-reaching and teaches an organic, gradual approach by which anybody can become truly healthy, completely free from any problem, by developing the universal thought of enlightenment.

Sometimes I ask my Western friends, "Do you have any enemies?" and they often reply that they do not; not one object of hatred. I say, "Really?" I don't believe them; I'm very skeptical. So then I ask, "Do you have any objects of desire; anything with which you're emotionally obsessed?" To that they usually reply, "Yes," to which I go, "Ah-ha!"

I respond like that because my studies of Buddhist psychology have taught me that if you have an object of grasping, emotional obsession you instinctively have objects of hatred; the mind of hatred is automatically there, waiting to react.

What do you think about that? Is my understanding polluted, wrong? What's the Western point of view? The Western mind is kind of radical…you're easy going; you think you don't have any enemies, but in fact you do. It's simply a matter of being aware. But we're usually not aware of what's in our mind.

From the Buddhist point of view, the healthy mind is one that is free of all objects of irritation—organic, inorganic, philosophy, ideology… anything. As long as your mind contains even one idea that makes you uneasy, you're neither free nor healthy.

Look at any big Western city these days. How many religious or psychotherapeutic groups are there? Do they all get along with each other or not? What about your own mind? Are you able to accept the trips that other people around you are on as necessary according to their individual need and simply let them be? Does something as simple as the noise of an airplane flying overhead upset you? Why? It comes; it goes. Don't get irritated; just let go. Airplanes are also individuals' need. If small things like that bother you, again, from the Buddhist point of view you're not mentally healthy.

Well, we can find many good examples of annoyance in twentieth century life. What about uranium enrichment, nuclear power stations or the recently announced neutron bomb[16]? Does your ego hurt when you hear the government announce such things? Do you react? Do you cry? There's no reason to react like that. It doesn't help. You're just making yourself emotionally sick, needlessly tiring yourself out. It's useless; we all know that.

Who knows? Perhaps President Reagan is a manifestation of Shakyamuni Buddha or Jesus Christ. I'm not lying. Intuitively, I can't say he's evil, so I can't say he's not buddha. It's not my business, either. You never know. I heard him explain the reality of the neutron bomb, how it

[16] The neutron bomb, which no longer exists, was a small thermonuclear weapon designed to harm mainly biological tissue. President Carter cancelled its development but President Reagan restarted it in 1981, around the time of this teaching.

destroys organic life and leaves all the precious inorganic resources intact. That's fantastic. Maybe it's a good thing. Perhaps this is another way of explaining the reality of Dharma, his way of explaining love. Perhaps human beings can learn love through this.

Sometimes the only way people can learn is through being shocked; if we don't get shocked we don't learn but remain comfortably in the dark shadow of ignorance. I believe that when we get a shock we learn; that that's the way to bring comprehension. Perhaps when people hear about the neutron bomb they'll develop detachment from their worldly possessions, thinking, "This bomb makes the entire future completely insecure. I might as well enjoy my wealth as much as possible because in a couple of months all my friends and I might have completely disappeared." Thus many people might develop detachment—how fantastic!

I often think that people don't pay attention when we explain the Buddhadharma because they're not shocked. They're kind of, "Oh, yeah… maybe yes, maybe no…." But when they hear about the bomb they think, "That's true. I'd better go to Hawaii for a holiday and have at least one week's good time. After that, whatever happens happens."

Since entering the monastery as a six-year-old I've heard about impermanence—how things are constantly changing, changing, changing— hundreds of times. But now, looking at this twentieth century world and seeing how quickly things change and react, I see impermanence more clean clear that I ever did and it really comes home to me how the Buddha was right. So that's unbelievably great. It's so clear.

Goodness! It seems that my teaching today has been mainly about the neutron bomb…you probably think I'm a complete disaster!

Well, this twentieth century life has advantages and disadvantages. One of the advantages is that we can get together and talk. If it weren't the twentieth century we wouldn't be here like this.

The wisdom of emptiness

The third principal aspect of the path is the wisdom of shunyata. In order to completely obliterate the root of human suffering we need to understand non-duality. Love, compassion, bodhicitta and other positive attitudes serve as temporary solutions to problems such as anxiety and the uncontrolled mind but they don't completely eradicate them; only the shunyata experience can do that.

Anyway, I'll explain these things in more detail as these teachings progress, so don't worry if you don't understand them right now.

Vajrayana

Tantrayana, or Mantrayana, means to elevate the consciousness, or liberate the mind, from ordinary thought. That's the connotation of mantra. The way we do this transformation is through the profound practice of deity yoga. Also, when we practice tantric meditations there's much emphasis on how to gain the experience of bliss, or pleasure.

Now, because Shakyamuni Buddha had complete realization—the fully omniscient wisdom that clearly knows the minds of all living beings, past, present and future—he was able to give a complete range of teachings, from the simplest up to the most profound, according to the level of mind of those in attendance. Therefore, within his teachings, we can find explanations of reality and methods for mental development suitable for us twentieth century seekers. Even 2,600 years ago the Buddha already knew us well and was able to leave us an appropriate, quick path to enlightenment.

As time passes, everything changes—culture, people's mentality and behavior, the environment and so forth—so the way that the teachings are presented also has to change. Today, when everything moves so fast, we can't necessarily use methods that in earlier times took a long time to accomplish. Lord Buddha himself said that when the culture changes, delusion, mentality and behavior also change, so even the *vinaya* rules have to be adjusted, because in their original form they may no longer benefit. We should therefore understand that Lord Buddha taught in order to help beings according to their individual need, so naturally, as time passes, the way his teachings are presented and practiced might also have to change. Even in times of nuclear war there'd still be a skillful way to practice Dharma.

If the teachings are not suited to the times and way of life, they're very difficult to practice. I mean, if the only way to reach enlightenment was to ride a snow lion around Amsterdam we'd really be in trouble.

However, the practice of tantra is very well suited to twentieth century life. Life today is full of pleasure but we also have a tendency to be easily confused and dissatisfied. Therefore we need a method whereby we can transform the energy of all our everyday life experiences into the path to enlightenment; we desperately need that kind of skill. So that's what tantra offers us.

Tantra doesn't emphasize renunciation and a negative view of life. In fact, in tantra we vow not to look at life negatively or to criticize our body. Tantra also doesn't allow us to place a higher value on men than women. Both men and women have an equal right to practice tantra in order to reach enlightenment and both men and women *can* reach the enlightenment of Shakyamuni Buddha in a single lifetime. Nevertheless, in some of his sutra teachings Lord Buddha did say that a male rebirth could be more advantageous than a female one and in certain times and environments I think that could be true.

Therefore I think Lord Buddha's tantra and sutra views are both correct; they both have reality because we're just talking about the superficial conventional view, not the absolute. For example, look at what ten-year-old children can do these days; things that even twenty-five year olds could not do in the past. It's amazing. The other day I saw a twelve-year-old girl on television doing things with a computer that most adults wouldn't have a clue about let alone be able to do.

Similarly, women can also do most things that men can do, too. I saw a female body-builder the other day...actually, she looked kind of grotesque! But I'm not saying it's bad. Human beings can do anything. Through Lord Buddha's teachings I've gained great confidence in people's potential and capabilities.

On the down side, however, I think people are more dangerous than any neutron bomb; one dissatisfied person can blow up the entire world. Anyway, the neutron bomb came from the human mind.

Still, the sophisticated modern energy people produce is very interesting. It's symbolic of the human mind, of modern culture. From the Buddhist point of view all those things are part of the human consciousness.

It's amazing. We're part of the neutron bomb. The non-duality of the neutron bomb is ours; our non-duality is that of the neutron bomb.

Anyway, the tantric viewpoint is that we should not criticize twentieth century life. Normally we complain about big-city life: "It's so crowded; it's so difficult; people are so angry and aggressive." That's our interpretation, but from the tantric point of view big cities are beautiful; tantra sees all the men and women of the city as Maitreya. Tantra leaves things as they are; city life as it is. Tantra says that everything, even worldly life, can be beautiful because it can all be experienced transcendentally by the human consciousness, unified by great universal love and non-duality.

After all, it's through the relative world that we discover absolute, ultimate reality, in the way that clouds are the source of good weather. If there are no clouds there's no good weather because good weather is what we get when the clouds disappear. In the way that the space of the sky allows the clouds to come and go, the space of non-duality allows the materiality of worldly life to function.

In a way, tantra reflects life in modern society because it emphasizes the enjoyment of as much pleasure as possible and discourages neglect of the body and living an ascetic life. In line with this, tantric meditations contain methods of exploding the pleasure centers in our *nadis*.

For example, many tantric meditators practice techniques where they concentrate at the heart. You might think, "I don't think so! My heart hurts enough already." You have the preconception that meditating at your heart will increase the pain you already feel. But that's not the way that yogis meditate. The purpose of meditating at the heart center is to generate an explosion of blissful pleasure there that satisfies the nervous system and eliminates craving for the outside world.

Then you might ask, "Why do we need physical transformation? Isn't it enough that we meditate with our mind?" From the tantric point of view the answer is no; we need physical transformation because we are physically dissatisfied, physically ignorant, physically angry. We are not only mentally disturbed but physically disturbed as well, and this kind of meditation is very powerful in knocking out our physical as well as our mental negativity.

When Western doctors test your reflexes they hit you just below the knee and your foot springs forward. They know something. Tibetan Buddhist tantra also knows something. If you build up energy in one part of your body, something happens in your head, something happens in your heart. So the practice of tantra also has the function of healing you physically as well as mentally.

The yoga method of Buddha Maitreya

The deity yoga we're talking about here is that of Maitreya. Iconographically, Maitreya has various aspects; in this sadhana, as a method of realizing our own profound reality body, we visualize ourselves in the aspect of the profound radiant light *sambhogakaya*, as beautiful as possible—super-beautiful, in fact; super-pure and just a super-magnificent transcendent object in general. In this way we eradicate our self-pity thoughts and self-pity imagination.[17]

At the moment we have two bodies existent within us—a physical body and a psychic, or conscious, body. So when we emanate as different deities we open the reality of other worlds, kind of like a flower opening. When a flower is closed it has certain shape; when it opens it has another.

From the tantric point of view, our grasping concepts of ego, which project a fixed, limited self-image of ourselves, are the main obstacle we need to overcome when trying to develop ourselves spiritually. And while our ego-concepts are the main enemy we have to vanquish, we have to get rid of our view of ordinary objects as well.

Our internal world is much deeper, much more profound, than that of our physical body, our bone, meat and skin. But even though our physical body is unbelievably limited, worth almost nothing, our ego thinks it's fantastic and forgets about our inner reality, which by comparison is like a universe.

As we know through experience, even normally we have hundreds of manifestations within us. For example, sometimes we get surprised by the arising of a profound aspect of ourself that we had no idea was in

[17] See *Introduction to Tantra*, chapter 11, for more on arising as a deity.

there, when we suddenly experience the deep comprehension of something we hadn't understood before. Or we can find ourselves shocked by the sudden manifestation of an ugly, self-pitying aspect of ourself that has us wondering where it possibly could have come from.

We've all experienced stuff like that, which is why I always say Buddhism is so natural, so humanistic. It simply talks about human experience. The profound things we experience come from within us, not from God. Buddhism says they're part of us.

The Buddhist approach is to introduce the human experience to show what great potential we have. That's all there is to it. It doesn't push us to try to attain something supernatural beyond our reach. That would be foolish. Buddhism doesn't proclaim, "This is supernatural; you've got to have it!" as if it were advertising a car: "If you don't buy this Mercedes you're a loser!"

Buddhism believes that human beings are like Buddha—human beings *are* Buddha—because we are capable of handling or putting an end to our own ego problems. We all have buddha-nature and should never think that we're worthless and buddhas are self-existent buddhas.

In fact, one of Lord Buddha's saying was, "Prostrate to the new moon, not the full one." Does that sound a bit strange? Actually, the idea is very important.

Buddhism doesn't value buddhas higher than human beings. We're considered as equal in value to Guru Shakyamuni Buddha, who completely transcended his ego and attained the state of eternal bliss. Buddhas and people are equal objects of prostration and respect, which is what Lord Buddha was getting at when he talked about prostrating to the new moon.

Instead of giving greater value and prostrating to buddhas and bodhisattvas, we should prostrate to the baby flowers that blossom into those beautiful big ones. That's logical, isn't it? If you want to enjoy a beautiful, fully developed flower you have to respect the baby flower it comes from. Human beings have buddha-nature and can solve any human problem.

In tantra, therefore, the emphasis is on meditation and how to develop transformation and gain transcendent experiences.

Perhaps I can explain it this way. Sometimes you're so clean clear and balanced inside that just by looking at you other people get some blissful energy; it's as if you were a buddha, where others gain pleasure just by seeing you. It happens. At other times you're so disturbed and your inner world is shaking so much that just by looking at you other people themselves magnetically feel shaken and disturbed. I'm sure you know this, too. It's simple.

These are good examples of transformation. Inner transformation makes a big difference to the outside world. Am I making myself clear? Sometimes you see another person who is so clean clear and blissful that you feel as if that person's blissful energy were shooting into you. I do; that's why I'm explaining it to you. These are good examples for practitioners of tantric yoga to think about.

Who is Maitreya?

Maitreya is the manifestation of the love of all the buddhas—the supreme beings who have achieved limitless, universal love. When we practice the yoga method of Buddha Maitreya we unify with the universal love energy that is Maitreya by developing to their ultimate extent the limited qualities of love, compassion and purity that presently lie within us.

To develop in this way we need to eliminate our self-cherishing thought; practice of the Maitreya yoga method is very powerful in allowing us to do this. Furthermore, this practice is of the utmost need today because the conditions of modern life overwhelm us emotionally and make us irritated with each other and desperately lonely as well.

This meditation course

This retreat is not some kind of intellectual Buddhist school. We're more interested in actualization and experience, so don't worry if you haven't understood everything I've been talking about. My main responsibility here is to explain the meditation we're going to do but I will gradually clarify some of the other things I've mentioned. So during these few days try to actualize as much as possible; try to gain some meditation experience of the practice.

In the next meditation session I want you to just relax and not be thinking, "I have to meditate." Don't think, "I have to meditate." Relax, but at the same time sit up straight so that your nervous system from neck to pelvis is not squeezed but clear and open.

Start by meditating on the breath. Again, don't think, "I have to do breathing meditation; I have to do breathing meditation." Stop thinking; just breathe. That's all you have to do; that's your only job. Again, don't think, "I have a job; I have to watch my breath." Don't think; just breathe with as few thoughts as possible.

However, generally saying "no thought" is not enough. It means no discursive, dualistic thought. Normally we have all these mental conversations…something comes into our mind and we go into a big story about it and it just goes on and on and on…. The purpose of meditating on the breath is to just naturally stop *that* kind of thought.

So that's the general meditation I'm suggesting everybody do, but if as an individual your mind is already clean clear, free of the emotional that-this kind of thought, I want you to contemplate on your own thought patterns.

And if you're somebody without meditation experience you can do the seed-syllable meditation, which even beginners can do.[18]

---

[18] See *How to Meditate*, "Inner Heat Meditation."

6. The Preliminaries

YESTERDAY YOU RECEIVED the Maitreya empowerment.[19] Today I'm going to explain how to approach enlightenment by practicing the yoga method of Maitreya.

The yoga method of Maitreya has two divisions: the preliminaries and the actual—or main body of the—meditation.

THE PRELIMINARY PRACTICES

The preliminary meditations for the yoga method of Maitreya are taking refuge and generating bodhicitta, cultivating the four immeasurables and generating special bodhicitta but it's not my job to describe them here.[20] However, why are they here in this text? Why are they a part of this practice?

The preliminaries are a kind of warning signal, like traffic lights, telling you to be careful. They show the beauty of Tibetan Buddhism; they're like an advertisement for Tibetan Buddhism. People nowadays are confused, both spiritually and in a worldly way, so what we need is a comfortable, step-like path to enlightenment, a process by which we can develop gradually, to ensure that our spiritual growth is natural and organic and that Dharma becomes us and we become Dharma.

Then the question may arise, "When practicing this sadhana, do we have to do the preliminaries every day?" They're here in the text; do you always have to do them? I'm going to say no, you don't. Then you're going

---

[19] For an example of an initiation given by Lama Yeshe see *Becoming Vajrasattva*, chapter 11, "An Initiation into Heruka Vajrasattva."
[20] See Appendix 2 for the Preliminary Practices section of the Maitreya sadhana.

to ask, "Well, why are they there?" to which the answer is that since we have to develop gradually, they're there to show us how to do that.

Refuge and bodhicitta[21]

If you already have complete confidence in Buddha, Dharma and Sangha—the supreme enlightened being and his wisdom teachings and feel that meditation practitioners are your best friends in the world—that's taking refuge. You don't have to recite the refuge formula, "I take refuge in Buddha, I take refuge in Dharma, I take refuge in Sangha," over and over. That way of taking refuge can be simply cultural and should be abandoned. Taking refuge is not verbal; there has to be something in your experience that leads you to feel that following the path shown by the Buddha is the way to gain complete liberation from suffering and you feel very comfortable with that. That's the essence of taking refuge.

The cultural way of taking refuge—going to the temple in the morning and mindlessly intoning the refuge formula—might be good for some people and better than the Western way of taking refuge each morning in coffee and the bathroom, but still, refuge should come intuitively; then you don't need words. The same goes for generating the enlightened attitude of bodhicitta—refuge and bodhicitta should both come intuitively, the way you want your morning coffee. When you're habituated to coffee you don't need to make an effort; your desire for coffee arises spontaneously. Similarly, when your mind is trained in refuge and bodhicitta, at a certain point you no longer need words.

The four immeasurables

The same goes for the four immeasurables. If you have eliminated strong feelings of attachment for your dear friends and hatred for your despised enemies and have equal feelings for all, you don't need to repeat the words. Verbal repetition is for those in whom the attitudes contained in

[21] See *Becoming Vajrasattva* for more detailed teachings on refuge and bodhicitta in the tantric context.

the four immeasurables have not become intuitive. We need words to bring comprehension but once we have developed understanding wisdom and the four thoughts arise intuitively, we don't need to meditate on them and we certainly don't need the words.

Special bodhicitta

Special bodhicitta is the enthusiastic desire to quickly, even more quickly, develop ourselves as much as possible, not just to overcome our own confusion but to benefit others in the highest way. For tantric practitioners, therefore, the main aim is not to get enlightened but to enlighten others.

The reason I emphasize this point is that sometimes people get the wrong impression that Tibetan Buddhism thinks that getting enlightened is the most important thing, like grasping at a piece of fruit. It's not at all like that.

Actually, you can understand the meaning from the words of the prayer. It says "for the sake of all mother sentient beings" not "for my sake." People tell me, "Lama, before I met the Dharma I used to strongly desire worldly pleasures but now I strongly desire enlightenment. This is what Buddhism seems to say." I agree; it's an understandable misconception to think that the goal of Mahayana Buddhism is to attain enlightenment for yourself rather than for all sentient beings.

But bodhicitta is profound, a universal attitude completely free of craving and grasping. The enlightened attitude of bodhicitta encompasses all living beings throughout all of space while functioning in the space of your own heart.

Then the question might arise: "I have complete confidence in Buddha, Dharma and Sangha, am fully convinced that this is my path, have had some success in meditation and in eliminating at least my gross mental problems, and feel love, compassion, bodhicitta and a feeling of equanimity for all living beings—isn't this enough?"

Isn't it enough to feel love for all sentient beings and have the universal thought that they all should reach enlightenment as quickly as possible? What more do we need? Isn't the practice of the preliminaries, which brings these results, enough? Why do we then need to progress to the main body of the Maitreya yoga method?

These are good questions and in a way it's true—through practicing the preliminaries we can eliminate extreme desire and hatred and gain a clear and peaceful mind, but that's *not* enough. Everyday emotions like hatred, jealousy, anxiety and so forth are merely symptoms arising from our ego, the root of all suffering, and until that is eradicated our spiritual growth will be stunted.

My scientific research into the Western world has opened my eyes; I see that Western religions also contain the preliminaries and value this kind of meditation. If you check the Bible wisely you'll find them there.

The difference in Buddhism, however, is that we also teach shunyata, which is something the West badly needs and why I feel that the Buddha's teachings are so useful for the Western mind. Only meditation on shunyata can eradicate the ego and that's why the actual meditation, the main body of the yoga method of Maitreya, begins with meditation on emptiness. Furthermore, the tantric process of becoming one with a deity such as Maitreya is also non-existent in Western religions and that's the principal meditation that we then go on to do.

Therefore I feel it's extremely worthwhile that Buddhadharma has come to the West; the need for these practices is great.

7. Meditation on Emptiness

THE MAIN BODY OF THE YOGA METHOD

Emptiness meditation

OM SVABHAVA SHUDDHA SARVA DHARMA SVABHAVA SHUDDHO HAM

I and all universally existent phenomena are recognized as non-duality.

(While reciting this mantra, contemplate on the non-dual nature of all phenomena, including yourself. Meditate upon the emptiness of inherent existence; then from the space of this emptiness arise as follows.)

The first thing in the actual yoga method is the shunyata meditation and it starts with the shunyata mantra in Sanskrit, OM SVABHAVA....[22]

OM means magnificent, unsurpassed quality
SVABHAVA means nature
SHUDDHA means fundamental purity
SARVA means all
DHARMA means phenomena—all existent phenomena
SVABHAVA SHUDDHO again means fundamentally pure nature
HAM means I am

---

[22] See Appendix 1 for another Lama Yeshe teaching on this mantra and a short meditation on emptiness.

That's very simple. Don't worry. The meaning of this mantra is very important.[23]

Our normal view of others and ourselves is mistaken, so this mantra is trying to set us straight. The Western scientific attitude in particular seems to have a very low opinion of what it means to be human. That's why they can so easily create something like the neutron bomb, which destroys people while leaving buildings intact. The message of the neutron bomb is that the value of property is supreme while that of human beings is nothing. OK, so now I'm definitely going to stop complaining about that!

However, this mantra is important because it talks about the quality of human nature, which we don't understand at all; our ego's concepts are artificial. The reason we meditate on shunyata is to become natural, to touch the fundamental reality of our own nature. So the *svabhava* mantra says that at their deepest nature, all existent phenomena, including ourselves, are inherently pure, not impure as our ego projects.

We're not talking philosophy or doctrine here; Buddhism does not propound some fabricated doctrine to make people feel better about themselves. This mantra states the way reality exists; it implies that the self-pity image of ourself held by ego is wrong. It's wrong because the fundamental nature of human beings is pure. We don't become pure through religious training, practicing pure morality and guarding our precepts carefully; we're naturally pure, not artificial.

Maitreya said, "Buddha-nature is like gold hidden beneath the earth." Dirt, rocks and stones are not of the nature of gold; the nature of gold is not dirt. Gold is gold. Similarly, the essence of human nature is pre-

---

[23] See also Lama Zopa Rinpoche's *Teachings from the Vajrasattva Retreat*, pp. 432–4 for further explanation of this mantra. And in Rinpoche's *tsa-tsa* commentary he says, "This is the *dharmakaya* meditation. Meditate that your own mind is the actual result-time dharmakaya of the deity you practice. If it is Maitreya, think: "This is my actual result-time Maitreya holy mind, the dharmakaya." This is the basic meditation according to the meaning of this mantra. Details of this meditation can be explained only after you have received a maha-anuttara initiation. There are three basic meditations: dharmakaya, sambhogakaya and *nirmanakaya*. This one is dharmakaya." See www.LamaYeshe.com.

cious and not that of disturbing emotions such as ego, hatred, jealousy and so forth.

It's very important that we recognize this because when we're overwhelmed by worldly problems we feel that we're a disaster by nature, that our nature is hopeless, ugly, impure and guilty. That's how we think whenever we're under the influence of our weak mind. When we're clean clear there's no way such thoughts can arise.

Why is this the case? If our deepest, most profound nature is so pure, how did it get so polluted? It's because of the artificial concepts of ego. Therefore, the practical thing to do is to investigate how our ego concepts imagine our self and the easiest way to do this is to examine our ego's moment-to-moment lifestyle—how it holds its preconceived imagination. By doing so we can come to understand how our ego drives our life.

If you're aware, your own experience will tell you that throughout your life you've repeatedly projected a preconceived imagination of yourself, and you can watch that nonsensical history in your mind and discover how ridiculous it is. When you do look at yourself like this you'll also discover that the way your ego holds its imagination of your self is totally non-existent; it's only an imaginary projection.

Furthermore, because the West emphasizes physical appearance, the Western ego develops thinking that the essential me is only body and has nothing to do with the mind.

The Buddhist point of view is that there's no way that the self can exist outside of the aggregates but when you search for it among the aggregates you still can't find it. No matter how deeply you peer into the cells of your body and examine all your atoms and neutrons, you can never find your self in there. But still, your ego thinks that the self must be in there somewhere.

Does this scare you? We always think, "I am so special, so dear," but when we search for our precious I we can't find it anywhere, on the collection of aggregates together or in any part of them divided. There's no self anywhere. Does this nihilistic idea scare you? It does me!

The Buddha once said something like, "The *dharmadhatu* has no words and neither subject nor object," and when this caused a disciple to express fear, he said, "The nature of fear is also dharmadhatu." What he meant was that fear is also non-dual in nature, so there's nothing to be afraid of.

Shunyata—ultimate reality—is to be found within all existent phenomena; it's simply a matter of discovering it. All conventional, relative phenomena are born with non-duality as their nature—they always have been and always will be. We have to understand and recognize that. That means that all phenomena have no self-entity; they are non-self in nature. As I explained before, when we search for a self in phenomena we can't find one, anywhere, like when we search the aggregates for the I.

For example, Paula exists only in name but our ego doesn't want to accept that. It wants to find the real Paula, the beautiful Paula, the wonderful Paula, the Paula who exists apart from the artificial name; it can't accept the Paula that's merely labeled on her aggregates; it wants *more* than that. It wants to find the self-existent beautiful Paula, which is totally non-existent. The ego always wants a concrete self. If it can't rely on a concrete Paula it thinks there's nothing there; if it can't grasp a concrete Paula it feels that Paula's non-existent.

You've heard shunyata translated as emptiness. What does this "empty" refer to? Normally it means if a glass is full of water and you tip it out, the glass is now empty. In Buddhist philosophy, what phenomena are empty of is self-existence, existence from their own side. There's no self-entity contained anywhere in or around Paula—that's what she's empty of. Her physical body is the container of Paula, but still her ego holds the self-notion of Paula. *That* is what's non-existent; that's what she's empty of.

Anyway, I'm not sure that the English word "emptiness" is the best way to translate shunyata because it gives the impression of loneliness: "My life is empty." Also, through misunderstanding the concept, many early Western professors concluded that Nagarjuna's philosophy was nihilistic, which is a wrong conception.

So now, a very simple, practical approach to understanding shunyata, to realizing the non-self-existent I, is first to just mindfully investigate how your ego holds the self-notion of your I, your self. That's the first thing to seek. Then, when at a certain point you discover that you're holding something heavy, solid, truly existent within you, a heavy concrete blanket, when through investigation you discover these hallucinated, nonsensical concepts, at the conclusion of this observation you can experience shunyata, non-conceptualization—let go and contemplate that.

In the superficial view of your ego, your self, or I, is something solid within either your body or your consciousness, but when you use wisdom and intensive awareness to investigate how your ego holds that self somewhere within your body or mind, you discover that there's no such solid, independent self anywhere. Contemplate on that discovery by remaining mindfully on the conclusion you have just reached and simply let go into that. That's the way to meditate.

Think of TV advertisements. First there's a loud, colorful commotion to get your attention, which then disappears as quickly as it came. The ego's a lot like that. First it puts on a big show, makes a big mess—the self-existent I is this big thing in the mind, at the heart or somewhere—but when you investigate, it too disappears.

Once when Lama Tsongkhapa was giving a teaching on emptiness one of his disciples, himself a great yogi, suddenly gasped and grabbed at his lapel because he'd completely lost his self; he thought he'd disappeared and got scared. Of course, his self soon re-appeared. This is a good example of what happens. He completely lost his concrete conception of ego, his entire mental universe disappeared, he thought he was becoming non-existent and to reassure himself that he was still there he grabbed at his shirt. That's the way to listen to your guru's teachings. We should all have such experiences in teachings and, because we have the intelligence to examine reality correctly, we can.

So in my opinion, the way to approach meditation on shunyata is to contemplate your own thoughts. Don't worry whether they're good or bad; at all times just be mindfully aware of whatever you're experiencing without engaging in discursive thought about either subject or object. Just contemplate.

Actually, I'm also not sure that "contemplate" is the right word here; you might not get my connotation. Similarly, I don't like the word "meditation" that much any more either, because these days people misunderstand that, too. However, irrespective of the word, at all times simply be aware of whatever you're experiencing, good or bad.

You have to be like a lamp. A lamp illuminates its surroundings without thinking, "I'm sending out light, brightening the area." It doesn't think anything, does it? It just is. That's how you contemplate. You're aware of what's going on but you don't react; you don't think, "Beautiful, good, bad," or anything. No conventional relationship or conversation. Just be aware. That's all. Even if bad thoughts come, don't react; their nature is clear as well. Bad thoughts are beautiful too; don't feel unpleasant when they arise.

Why do we meditate like this? Because it helps us with our non-conceptual discovery of shunyata, universal reality. How? Because it's our consciousness that experiences the moment and the nature of our consciousness is always clear; when we're clear we can see the games our ego plays, how it holds the notion of a self-I. Our ego's very cunning; if we don't meditate with intensive awareness it can easily escape our attention but if we apply intensive awareness to mindfulness of our own experience, we can catch our ego's concepts and realize them as nonsense.

All our experiences are mental energy; all experiences are consciousness. And the nature of consciousness is always natural, always clear, irrespective of how confused we are.

So the emphasis of today's meditation has to be on shunyata. I want you to research how your ego reacts every minute; you can learn every time it does. When your ego's not reacting it's in hiding.

The ego is not something intellectual; it's totally an innate part of our nature; we were born with it and it's been with us ever since. Therefore, in order to eradicate the concepts of ego we have to meditate with the clearest and most refined levels of mind; without meditation we can't completely destroy our ego's deep roots. Our ego is very intelligent, clever, manipulative and elusive. For that reason, students in Lama Tsongkhapa's tradition are sometimes told to search the whole world for the self-existent I.

There's a story that once a lama told one of his young incarnate lama disciples very seriously, "You definitely have a self-existent I; I want you to look for it everywhere…it must be somewhere, on the plains or in the mountains. You have to find it." So this young lama took his teacher's advice literally and ran around the whole day looking for his self-existent I. That night he came back to the monastery exhausted and very disappointed at not having found it. We all laughed a lot when we heard that.

Still, I don't think it's a bad idea to make looking for the self-existent I a full-time job. Sometimes we're not serious in our practice; we don't take it as a job. When you have a job, you do it; you act. That's good. So your job today is to check out your ego and how it holds preconceived ideas about yourself. Decide, "Yes, today my practice is my job." That's the way to make your practice sincere.

Of course, there's no such thing as physically running about searching for your ego—that's just a metaphor. Instead, what you have to do is to place intensive awareness on the energy of your own experience, to continuously keep your mind on whatever you're experiencing, to remember it constantly. When you get distracted, practice mindfulness of breathing; when that clears your mind, go back to awareness of experience.

Q: I find it difficult to search for the I in all the parts of my body because you've already said we won't find it.

Lama: Well, I gave you merely the intellectual answer; now you have to *experience* it. Actually, this is an important question. That's why the Gelug tradition has its students running about everywhere looking for the self-existent I. When I first heard this I thought they were just playing games but then I checked further; they're not stupid. You have to get your answers through experience, don't you? It's not an intellectual thing. Then I felt grateful; this is serious, not hypocritical. Getting introduced to the non-self-existent I directly in this way makes it a very powerful experience. That's why I told you yesterday that during this meditation course we're more interested in experience than theory. In that way we help each other. That's the main point.

So, when you've had the experience of not finding the self-existent I, whenever your ego reacts emotionally you can apply that experience to everyday life. That's the way you become buddha.

Q: What's the relationship between the individual mindstream, which always exists, and the self-existent I, which does not exist at all?

Lama: There's no self-existent continuity of consciousness whatsoever, just as there's no self-existent I. Neither is there any self-existent God, Buddha or Dharma. That's the beauty of Lord Buddha's teaching. There's no exception, like, Buddha is self-existent but everything else is not. Lord Buddha himself said that sort of talk is rubbish. All phenomena in the universe are one in the total unity of non-duality. That's what we mean when we say that samsara and nirvana are the same thing. This is the beauty of Lord Buddha's psychology—its main concern is for the suffering sentient beings who hold onto the extreme of the self-existent I, thinking, "These [self-existent] six paramitas are fantastic! God is fantastic!" Lord Buddha says such thoughts are rubbish, symptoms of a sick mind.

In other words, Lord Buddha negated all self-existence; in his *Perfection of Wisdom* sutras he said that there's nothing that's self-existent—samsara, nirvana, enlightenment…anything. It's not possible. That's why his teachings are so profound, so universal. There's no emphasis on something special; reality is completely universal. Lord Buddha wanted people to be perfectly healthy so he didn't want any partial, self-existent object appearing to the human mind.

However, from the moment of conception, our relative mind and our ego's view have continued, changing, changing, changing—just not in a self-existent way.

Q: Which part of the mind is it that recognizes or sees non-duality?
Lama: Awareness—which is always with you, always there. It's simply a matter of developing it. For example, you have love and compassion within you right now but you need to make them bigger and better. So when we practice Buddhism it's not as if we're trying to acquire something that we don't already have. Something is there; we believe that humans do have love, compassion and wisdom. It's simply a question of developing them to their ultimate potential.

8. Becoming Maitreya

Meditation

W HY DOES BUDDHISM put so much emphasis on meditation? It's because our mind is so gross and our memory so poor that we forget things easily and cannot recall our countless lives' experiences. The purpose of meditation, therefore, is to increase, or develop, our memory, or mindfulness, of reality.

Our distracted, fragmented thoughts, which we experience continuously every day, are countless. Nonsense repeatedly cycles through our mind, again, again, again, again.... It's like in the pictures of the wheel of life, whose hub shows a pig, a chicken and a snake going round and round endlessly. Like that, our pig, chicken and snake mentalities continuously reverberate in our consciousness, reducing our memory to almost nothing.

The meditation techniques that stop these three mentalities are very important. Without stopping these deluded minds we can't see the concepts of ego that we spontaneously experience in everyday life. They're very subtle, so without eliminating these gross minds it's impossible to see our ego's activity. That's why we meditate on the energy of our own conscious experience. By quieting and eliminating our gross mentalities we create the space we need to see the concepts of ego, to recognize the entity interpreted by ego, which is non-existent.

Normally, religious people miss the point—we circle around it but don't make much progress because we keep missing it. What is the point? The point is to become revolutionaries and totally destroy our entire concepts of ego. This is a much more revolutionary ideal than any of the theories propounded by Marx-Lenin, Hitler or Mao.

The concepts of ego project an independent, self-existent I totally unrelated to physical matter, time, space, cause, effect or anything else, existing somewhere, untouchable. Our ego holds on to the self-existent I and never lets it go.

Based on the results of his own practice, Lama Tsongkhapa said that by contemplating our conscious experience we can cut our superstitious, dualistic thoughts and thereby discover our ego projections and realize shunyata in a flash. Like throwing a switch, the moment we discover exactly what the false conception is, at that instant we discover non-duality.

The most difficult thing to recognize is the entity held by our ego, and the only way to do this is to meditate. According to Lama Tsongkhapa there's no way to do it intellectually. To prove this, he quoted Nagarjuna: "The person is not of the nature of earth, water, fire, air, space or even consciousness. The person exists only as a conventional designation." Lama Tsongkhapa totally agreed with Nagarjuna: all phenomena exist only in name. So we should just leave things as they are—superficial names projected by superstition—and not try to find some real, self-existent entity beyond that.

Some people think that first we have to study shunyata in order to understand it and then meditate. That's wrong. To realize shunyata, first we have to meditate.

The thing is that the gross symptoms of ego, the three poisonous mentalities I just mentioned, disturb, irritate and shake the mind, so without subduing them to a certain extent—and there are various levels to which they can be subdued—there's no way to see the unconscious levels of ego that hold the notion of an independent self-existent I. It's impossible. And that's the point. Therefore our approach has to be through meditation—the experience of contemplating the energy of mental clarity automatically eliminates those mentalities.

Otherwise, it's like Lama Tsongkhapa said—our enemy's hiding out in the jungle but we're looking for him in town. That's us—we practitioners are always busy doing something religious but never get anywhere because we miss the point and look for our ego in completely the wrong place.

Therefore it's very important to stop our "that-this" superstitious thoughts and we're capable of doing so. By simply remaining mindfully aware of the experience of our own energy without getting involved either subjectively or objectively in that-this thinking, focusing our mind and letting go, we'll no longer have a problem with distraction.

It's similar to our present situation. We're here in this peaceful Dharma center knowing that there are disasters and bloodshed happening all over the world but not getting emotionally disturbed. It's like that.

When I say "let go" I mean to focus on the clarity of mind and just remain there without expectation or emotional conversation. As I mentioned before, when the full moon shines it doesn't have any expectation or thoughts such as "I'm illuminating the Earth." It doesn't think anything; it just illuminates. The fewer dualistic thoughts you have, the greater the peace, tranquility, satisfaction and bliss you experience—and satisfaction and bliss are antidotes to dissatisfaction, depression, aggression, distraction and all other emotional disturbances.

When we meditate on an object with continuous, focused attention, our sense perception no longer functions. In other words, we go beyond sense perception. Sense perception has a bad reputation in Buddhism because it's the door to delusion and superstition. Whatever our senses perceive is always an optical illusion; the nature of sense perception is such that it produces more ego and superstition.

Therefore meditators deem the sense world unimportant. Since whatever appears to their sense perception is illusory, they no longer trust or use it much, but Maitreya also emphasizes in his writings that the mind the meditator uses is the sixth, or mental, consciousness, which is not sense perception or sense consciousness.

When a fighter pilot first sees an enemy plane it might be a long way off but as that self-existent plane gets closer and closer he sees it more and more clearly and at a certain point can shoot it down. The moment it disappears he experiences a kind of emptiness, shunyata. Similarly, when our clear wisdom first tries to find our ego, it's not very obvious; it's hiding. But as our concentration deepens our ego finds it increasingly difficult to remain out of sight and eventually it appears right there in front of us. As soon as we recognize it we should destroy it, and the moment it disappears we experience shunyata. The nuclear missile we use to shoot down our self-existent I is mindfulness, the wisdom of intensive awareness, and we don't need dualistic thought to pull the trigger; the moment our ego appears, we shoot it down.

When we reach the point of experiencing the non-dual I in this way, we should just let go and focus on our mind with clear comprehension. Also, the "non" in non-dual shouldn't make us feel lonely: "I feel so empty, I have no dear friend." To experience non-duality is to experience the universe. We should feel, "I am the reality of all universal phenomena," or "The reality of all universal phenomena is me."

But again, these are not conceptual thoughts. What I'm talking about is pure experience, what we call the enlightened, or dharmakaya, experience and, in a way, we can say it's the experience of the omnipresent love and wisdom of Maitreya.

However, the dharmakaya experience is invisible, and in order to communicate with sentient beings we have to emanate in a visible form.

Emergence from emptiness

In the empty space of non-duality
Appear eight mighty snow lions
Supporting a precious jeweled throne
Upon which rests a lotus and moon disc.
And upon this vast, white moon disc
My mind manifests as a syllable HUM [or MEM],
Brilliant golden light, the size of a sesame seed.

(Let your mind sink into this syllable completely and try to contemplate without differentiation of subject and object. You are this golden syllable HUM.)

From the space of non-duality, or non-conceptualization, your consciousness manifests as a fresh, new lotus flower in the center of which your wisdom manifests as a full moon disc. At the center of the moon disc, the essence of your consciousness manifests as a brilliant golden light syllable HUM and the vibrating sound HUMMMM. At the same time the sound of the Maitreya mantra automatically fills all of space.[24]

Accomplishing the two purposes

From this syllable
Radiant light shines out in all ten directions
Making offerings of exquisite beauty to all buddhas and
    bodhisattvas
And then purifying the negative energy of all sentient beings,
Leading them to the state of enlightenment.
Once these two purposes have been accomplished
This light dissolves back into my mind.

Golden light radiates from the syllable HUM at your heart throughout all of space making offerings to all the buddhas and bodhisattvas and touches all sentient beings, purifying them of all their hatred and giving them eternal satisfaction. It then returns and sinks back into the syllable HUM. Concentrate strongly on your unity with this golden syllable, which is your consciousness, your psyche. This golden light is you; you are this golden light.

Self-generation

Instantly
I become Maitreya Buddha,
With a clear light body, golden in color,
With one face and two arms.
My two hands are poised at my heart
In the mudra of turning the wheel of Dharma
In each hand I hold the stem of a lotus;

---

[24] There are several Maitreya mantras. The one that Lama explained during this teaching is OM AH MAITRI SARVA SIDDHI HUM, perhaps because it is short and therefore easier to visualize and recite. See Appendix 3 for the usual root, heart and near-heart mantras.

Upon the right is a wheel; upon the left is a vase.
My black hair is pulled back and tied in a knot
And my head is crowned with a stupa of enlightenment.
My face wears a smiling, peaceful expression
And my body is adorned with the eighty qualities
And thirty-two marks of magnificence.
Precious ornaments decorate my body
And I emanate an aura of five-colored light
As I am seated in the majestic position
With my feet planted firmly upon the ground.
Three syllables adorn my body:
A white OM at my crown,
A red AH at my throat
And a blue HUM at my heart.

All of a sudden this golden light, your consciousness, transforms into Maitreya. Your body is made of reddish-golden radiant rainbow light and is huge, like 100,000 feet high. It is made of pure light and contains not an atom of physical matter. You are very youthful looking, have one face and two arms, and can be either sitting in the vajra posture or in a chair.[25] Since you have conquered the enemy of ego with universal love, your essence is universal love and compassion. Completely unify with the enlightened nature of Maitreya and generate divine pride: "I *am* Maitreya, in the nature of universal love and compassion; I *am* the liberator of the universe." Completely identify with Maitreya, the enlightened one. With focused awareness of yourself as the emanation of Maitreya, let go.

At this point spend time meditating on emptiness and the process of generating yourself as Maitreya. Actualize these two as much as you can.

So, let's finish here for now, but are there any questions?

---

[25] The sadhana mentions visualizing yourself as Maitreya seated on a chair-like throne, which symbolizes his being the next buddha, ready to get up and descend to Earth to turn the wheel of Dharma. As Lama says, you can also visualize yourself as Maitreya in the more usual vajra posture, or what is often called the full lotus.

Q: Is it possible to be aware of awareness?

Lama: Yes, but just *be* awareness, that's all. Don't conceptualize, "I'm awareness; I'm awareness." Just let go. It's like driving a car; when you drive you don't have to keep thinking, "I'm a driver; I'm a driver." Just drive; just *be* a driver. New drivers get all caught up in "I'm a driver" and that's how accidents happen.

Q: I understand the word "meditation" and the importance of meditating but I have a problem when you talk about sensory experience. Some lamas teach that you should meditate by opening your senses and looking around because if you really use all your senses you can become more consciousness and aware of what you're doing and what's around you. Does this contradict what you're saying?

Lama: They might be talking about meditators on a higher level. If you have the penetrative wisdom that directly knows sense objects the way they are, it's OK to meditate like that. If you have wisdom you can be looking at a flower and at the same time be going beyond it, beyond the sense perception—the flower is so beautiful; just looking at it propels you further along the path to enlightenment. But if you don't have that kind of wisdom, looking at sense objects can just make you even more bananas than you already are.

Q: But don't you have to see sense objects well before you can go further?

Lama: No. My point is that if you don't have wisdom, you can be looking at something through your senses but not be aware of its reality. We're in contact with the sense world all the time—looking, tasting, touching—but we're never aware of, never touch, its reality. All we see is the superficial bubble.

Q: Can one have a negative experience after doing the meditation on emptiness because of being ignorant of what's happening?

Lama: It's possible, because if you try to stop all thought but don't have intensive awareness, you can end up with a heavy, sluggish, sleepy mind. Anyway, there are many teachings on the various hindrances to meditation, like sluggishness and distraction, and how to overcome them, and if you study those you will have a much better idea of how to make your meditation positive.

Q: How about the opposite situation, where you get too much energy from meditation?

Lama: Then the excess energy needs to be released. You need to find a way of directing it into the path to enlightenment.

9. Meditation on Maitreya

Divine pride

W HEN WE BECOME MAITREYA we have to be really convinced that we're the real thing rather than think that we're just pretending. Pretence is no good; we need to really believe "I *am* the universal love and compassion that is Maitreya." Remember, Maitreya isn't just some person. "I am Maitreya" is actually the experience of enlightenment.

This method of bringing the experience of enlightenment into the present is unique to tantra. It's a radical expression. When we think, "I am the experience of universal love and compassion," which is the essential characteristic of Maitreya, we knock out all our self-pity thoughts and imagination, and the more we develop that thought the more we eradicate our self-pity.

In a way, it's like thinking, "At the moment, I'm a profound, healthy, modern man, a profound, healthy, modern woman, functioning perfectly in modern society." Carl Jung spoke a lot about modern man. I interpret that to mean enlightened man...or woman. Don't think he didn't include women when he said that. Men and women can do *anything*; we are equally capable of *anything*.

Why am I bringing this up? If we're under the influence of our ego-created preconceptions and think, "I can't do this; I can't do that. Modern men and women have to be like this—that's beyond me," you're lying to yourself. It's not true; it's the wrong attitude.

I have a lot of hippie students in Australia. They wear rags, don't use make-up, go barefoot and live in isolated areas. I find it very beautiful. When I went back to Australia earlier this year I got a big shock: their hair was clean, they were wearing make-up and nice, modern clothes like everybody else. They looked like Hollywood movie stars. I said, "Do you enjoy being like this?" They said, "Yes, very much." I thought great; let them go.

Before, they were very confrontational; if somebody looked at them the wrong way they'd get upset. Now they're completely different. I was very surprised. When I first met them they wouldn't dream of working; now they all have jobs, make lots of money, go to fancy restaurants for lunch and dinner and love dancing. Of course, they're not gods; they're just like us.

I feel they're being realistic. I like my Western students to be normal Westerners and take advantage of what society has to offer. Conventionally they're imitating other people but what's the big deal? We can imitate anything we like.

If we look at it from the Dharma point of view, imitating others can be likened to manifesting as Maitreya. Why manifest as Maitreya? Lord Buddha manifested in many different ways. At certain times it was appropriate for him to manifest in a certain aspect, so he did. We can be like that, too. If, in a certain environment, it's appropriate for us to manifest in a certain way, we can do so, and in that way our energy can remain in harmony with our surroundings.

Lord Buddha's sutra teachings assert that the root of samsara, the cause of all suffering, is ignorance, in particular the self-grasping ignorance that is the ego. From the tantric point of view, the root of samsara is the ordinary conception, or view, of seeing ourselves as poor quality; tantra considers the self-pity image to be the main obstacle to human progress. This assertion is unique to tantra.

Therefore we have to transform ourselves into, or emanate as, Maitreya, with a golden radiant-light body and the strong conviction, "I am Buddha Maitreya," and it's very important that we develop this kind of understanding wisdom.

Practicing in this way is very logical and very simple. For example, look at the way Western society has developed. Twenty-four hours a day, advertising is telling us, "Men should be like this; women should be like that. Put this here; don't put that there. This is bad; that is good." It's all so incredibly aggressive; we're constantly bombarded by dualistic images of "this is better, that is worse; this looks good, that looks bad" so that in our mind we come to really believe what they're telling us and start acting in the way they want.

In a way, we have no choice. Western society is so proud of its great democratic and individual freedoms but they're illusory. Actually, our ego is always put into a very narrow position. Is Western society mad or not? Well, it's our own emanation—we abandon our natural body and kind of create an artificial one. We do this to ourselves; Tibetan Buddhism doesn't do it to us.

It's strange, isn't it? When we look at ourselves and our situation through the lens of Lord Buddha's teaching we can laugh at ourselves; we can be sitting here quietly and suddenly burst out laughing. That's the power of the Dharma. It's strange, yet for me it's completely logical. Why do contemporary men and women change the shape of their body? It's because of desire and grasping.

Clear appearance

As far as the technique of self-generation is concerned, we do need to generate a clean clear mental image of Maitreya's golden radiant light body but at first it's quite gross. That's good enough. We don't need to see the details of his eyes, nose and so forth. First we just try to get a total picture in our mind and contemplate that with mindfulness and clarity, without distraction or sluggishness.

One meditation technique that can help make concentration and mindfulness easier is to breathe in slowly and gently and hold it, which helps bring energy inside. But don't force it; as soon as it becomes uncomfortable to keep holding your breath, exhale.

When you exhale it's important to do so slowly and completely otherwise too much pressure builds up in your body. Holding your breath is good for developing concentration but failing to exhale properly can block the flow of energy and cause pain.

Build up your concentration on the emanation of yourself as Maitreya slowly and without expectation. It's a gradual process. When you have a general impression of yourself as Maitreya, rest in mindful awareness of that without intellectualizing and just let go. Then, to develop continuous concentration, mindfulness and awareness, inhale and hold, which will make your visualization more clear.

Holding your breath can also help to control your emotional bodily reactions. Our bodily emotions are often unstable and give others a false impression, which can be a big problem in human relationships. We need to develop stability and control over them.

Breath movement is important. Sometimes we see mentally disturbed people breathing rapidly and noisily. From the Tibetan Buddhist point of view, when the mind is refined so too is the breath.

Having developed clear appearance of yourself as the deity you then need to generate divine pride, as above. Develop divine pride and clear appearance alternately. When mindfulness of yourself as Maitreya is strong, pour on the gasoline of divine pride: "I am the universal love energy of Maitreya." When this is strong, let go. When you need to make your concentration stronger, generate more clarity of your visualization and when you have done so, again let go. Then, at a certain point, generate divine pride once more: "I *am* universal love and compassion."

Alternating in this way, build up the two factors of clarity and divine pride. This is the way to train your mind. Generate the intensive awareness of concentration. When your mind stops moving, simultaneously generate divine pride. Make it stronger and again let go. Then make your concentration stronger—more light, more clarity, then let go. When there's no distraction, leave it there and simultaneously add the gasoline of divine pride without moving or disturbing your concentration.

As I said before, it's a bit like driving a car. You drive along with concentration and mindfulness and change gears without thinking, spontaneously. It's no big deal; it's automatic.

The object of the divine pride you generate should be the unity of the universal love energy of Maitreya's clear light body and non-duality. The unity of these two is of the nature of enlightenment and "that is me." When you say, "I am the enlightened state of Maitreya," you have to understand that there's a basis of reality to the divine pride you generate.

When you see yourself possessing the profound, transcendent qualities of Buddha Maitreya, divine pride is extremely effective in eliminating self-pity pride, the pride of being inferior. The qualities with which you identify should be profound—"Non-duality is me; I am non-duality"—and when, on the basis of these profound qualities, you develop concentration on the crystal-clear, rainbow body of Maitreya, it's easy to discover shunyata because you're aware of its non-dual nature.

The main thing in developing concentration is to continuously remember the object on which you're focused without sluggishness or distraction. To help with this you need to develop the skill of recognizing negative thoughts that arise during meditation as the energy of universal love. If you can do this you leave no room for negative thoughts to proliferate. That's also a technique for eliminating distraction; you can deal with other distractions in a similar way: recognize distracting sounds as mantra and distracting pleasures in the nature of blissful non-dual wisdom.

These things are very important when you practice the main body of the yoga method. If you practice in this way, real transformation will come.

Mantra recitation

From the practical point of view, when practicing sadhanas, recitation of the mantra is not the main thing. First you have to develop clear appearance and divine pride of yourself as the deity. Mantra practice follows that. Once you have developed strong concentration and divine pride, without losing concentration, shift your focus and meditate on the syllable HUM and moon disc at your heart. Unify your mind with the moon disc—your mind becomes the moon disc—and meditate for a short time on that.

Then, at the center of the moon disc, a golden light syllable HUM appears, with the mantra OM AH MAITRI SARVA SIDDHI HUM standing clockwise around the periphery of the moon disc, and this is when you can recite the mantra.

As you do, much radiant light emanates from the syllable, mantra, moon and your body, pervading the ten directions of the universe, touching all living beings. They are all purified of whatever sufferings and dissatisfaction they have—physical, mental, emotional—and transformed into Maitreya—all living beings appear as Maitreya, all sound as mantra and all thoughts as universal love and wisdom. Then, all beings, in the aspect of Maitreya, sink into you. This improves your concentration.

You can also recite the mantra silently. First recite it with sound, then without; do mental recitation. When your concentration on this is good you can move to practice other techniques.

For example, you are Maitreya and on the moon disc at your heart is a small flame, or the feeling of fire. Your consciousness manifests within this fire feeling as the mantra; in aspect it's the mantra but in essence it's your consciousness. So, when you practice this technique, don't recite the words of the mantra; just concentrate on the unity of the fire, the mantra and your non-dual wisdom. Hold this mindfully, without distraction or sluggishness, emphasizing the unity of *vipashyana* meditation.

Again, in order to enhance clear concentration when practicing these meditation techniques, breathe in and hold it without exhaling quickly.

The effect of practicing these particular meditation techniques is the experience of great bliss and non-superstitious wisdom, similar to *tummo* meditation, which also produces heat and blissful energy in your nervous system.[26]

Once you have mastered that meditation with good concentration and the desired effects, again shift your emphasis. On the moon disc at your heart visualize another very subtle, very small Maitreya. His size can be according to what works best for you: like a sesame seed or a little bigger, like a rice grain or even an apple. It depends on your own experience but make him as small as you can. And then, again, at his heart concentrate on the fire feeling and mantra. This trains your mind to become very subtle and helps you reach the very depths of your unconscious mind.

There are other techniques you can employ but I think that's enough

---

[26] See Lama's *Bliss of Inner Fire*.

for now. I hope you don't feel deprived of meditations to practice. However, the techniques I have given you very briefly here are actually very powerful and are what you need to practice to develop special insight.

Transforming yourself into Maitreya is very important. It changes your entire mental attitude. For example, when you see a normal rainbow you don't grasp at it strongly or get neurotic and emotionally disturbed. Since your attitude toward it is different from how you normally relate to sense objects, your relationship with it changes too; your feelings and emotions change. Similarly, by transforming yourself into the profound, universal love characteristic of Maitreya, you can easily change your attitudes, feelings and emotions and easily understand non-duality.

The posture in which you visualize yourself as Maitreya can be as seated on a chair, as mentioned in the sadhana, or in the vajra posture, whichever you feel more comfortable with. And your three places are marked by OM, AH and HUM.

Now let's return to the sadhana where we left off.

Invocation of the wisdom beings

> From the blue HUM at my heart
> Much brilliant blue light radiates out to Tushita,
> Invoking the wisdom beings in the form of Maitreya,
> Who come back with the light and melt into me.
>
> *(Generate the strong divine pride that you have actually become Maitreya Buddha and visualize yourself vividly as having a brilliant form made of clear light, as transparent as crystal.)*

What is the purpose of doing this? You are Maitreya but there's also the Maitreya who we normally think of, the relatively existent Maitreya in Tushita pure land. *He* is a wisdom being. So the question arises, since we've already become Maitreya, why do we need to invoke an external one? It's because we still have our dualistic mind and it's always out of control. We always see things dualistically. Invoking the wisdom beings from Tushita or the ten directions in the aspect of

Maitreya and having them enter and unify with us helps us overcome that dualistic view.

As the text says: "Generate the strong divine pride that you have actually become Maitreya Buddha and visualize yourself vividly as having a brilliant form made of clear light, as transparent as crystal."

The emphasis of this yoga method is putting an end to all dualistic thinking, so we generate the shunyata experience and arise as Maitreya, but still within us, perhaps even unconsciously, there's a feeling of separation: "I'm the self-pity one; Maitreya is fully enlightened universal love, wisdom and compassion." The experience of invoking and absorbing the wisdom beings helps cut the dualistic thought that sees us as separate from the wisdom being Maitreya.

10. Concluding Practices

Offerings to oneself as Maitreya

(a) Removing interferences

(Recite the following mantra while visualizing that all impure ener-
gies—particularly those deriving from the mistaken view of inherent
existence—are chased away from the objects of offering.)

OM VAJRA AMRITA KUNDALI HANA HANA HUM PHAT

(b) Dissolution into emptiness

OM SVABHAVA SHUDDHA SARVA DHARMA SVABHAVA SHUDDHO HAM
Everything becomes empty

(c) Transformation and blessing

All the offerings are recognized as non-duality,
Yet manifesting in the form of the individual offerings
And functioning to elicit the experience of bliss
As objects to be enjoyed by all the six senses.

(The elaborate visualization can be done as follows. The eight objects
of offering dissolve into emptiness, from which the eight syllables OM
appear. These transform into offering bowls each containing the syllable
HUM. *The* HUMs *dissolve into light and transform into the individual*
objects of offering. Then visualize that above each offering bowl are the

syllables OM, AH *and* HUM *in ascending order. Recite the following eight blessing mantras. As you recite* OM, *white light radiates from the syllable above the first offering into the ten directions of space and draws the enlightened quality of the holy body of all buddhas and bodhisattvas back into the* OM, *which then sinks into the offering bowl. In a similar fashion, red light from the* AH *and blue from the* HUM *draw back the enlightened qualities of the speech and mind of these holy beings. In this way all eight offerings are transformed and blessed.)*

OM ARGHAM AH HUM

OM PADYAM AH HUM

OM... etc..

(d) Presentation of the offerings

(While reciting the following offering mantras and performing the appropriate mudras, visualize offering goddesses emanating from your heart, presenting the offerings to yourself as Maitreya Buddha and then dissolving back into your heart.)

OM ARYA ARGHAM PRATICCA HUM SVAHA... (etc.)

After invoking the wisdom beings and again generating clear appearance and divine pride, we bless all the sense objects in the universe and offer them to ourself as Maitreya. We can also offer these objects of enjoyment to other beings, seeing them as Maitreya as well.

The offerings are blessed and purified because if we view them dualistically they're impure and therefore not worthy of offering. Thus we have to recognize all the objects we offer as non-dual in nature.

The significance of offering is not simply giving. The way we usually give has no significance; it's just part of our normal ego game. Giving the tantric way involves total transformation. That's what a *mandala* means: it signifies totality. Everything that exists is transformed; this is not some half-half practice. We transform every possible enjoyment into the blissful, everlasting energy of the non-superstitious wisdom of Maitreya and then make the offering. By recognizing ourself as an enlightened being and the enjoyments we offer as the energy of transcendent, non-dual wisdom, everything we do becomes the path to enlightenment.

For example, normally when we eat and drink we don't do so with appreciation. Some people are obsessed with food and eat too much. Others think eating is a hassle, negative; they think that eating is animal behavior. It doesn't have to be that way; we can eat with respect and appreciation. When we recognize food as the energy of universal love and wisdom, each mouthful brings the experience of blissful energy, which increases our satisfaction. Increasing satisfaction in this way increases our wisdom. It is very powerful. The enjoyment of eating depends more on the relationship we have with our food—the attitude with which we eat—than on the amount of food we consume. If we eat with a bad feeling we get a bad effect; if we eat with a good attitude we get a good result. Eating with superstition can automatically produce a stomach ache.

Anyway, we know from everyday life that if we eat with a negative mind, even if we completely stuff ourselves, we don't find satisfaction, only more dissatisfaction, whereas if we eat with a reasonable attitude, even a small amount of food can satisfy us, both physically and mentally.

One reason for the increasing incidence of cancer in the West is that we eat without appreciation. We appreciate money but not food. I'm not going to say much on this but that's what produces cancer. Before the industrial revolution there wasn't much cancer because people's hunter-gatherer attitude to food was much more appreciative and more in harmony with nature. Now there's no relationship between nature, people and the food we eat. Even you and I don't have a proper relationship. Everything's so dualistic.[27]

Take electricity, for example. Without it, city people would die, wouldn't they? Anyway, they'd be in trouble. On the other hand, as I read in *Readers Digest* recently, high voltage electricity can damage the body. I don't know if this is true but it could be. However, I'm getting off topic here.

The main point I'm trying to make is that we have to transform our

---

[27] For more of Lama's opinion on all this, see *Becoming Vajrasattva*, pages 168 and 196.

entire environment—mountains, houses, our body, all sense objects, everything—into a reflection of transcendent, blissful wisdom and recognize its non-dual and clear light nature. This method cuts our ordinary ego concepts and view, so it's very important.

I think the rest of the sadhana is fairly self-evident.

Praise

(Thinking deeply about the excellent qualities of Maitreya Buddha, recite the following prayer)

I pay homage and offer praise to Maitreya Buddha
Who, by accomplishing the meditation of loving-kindness,
Has conquered all enemies and harm: the negative forces of
Mara,
And cares for all mother sentient beings with great compassion.

Recitation of the mantra

(With strong concentration visualize the following as clearly as possible.)

At my heart is a moon disc
Upon which rests the golden syllable HUM [or MEM]
Surrounded by the glowing letters of the mantra:
OM AH MAITRI SARVA SIDDHI HUM.

From these much brilliant light radiates in all ten directions
Filling the entire universe and purifying all negative energy
—Just as the rays of the sun instantly eliminate darkness—
And leading all beings to the state of Maitreya Buddha.

Again light radiates forth in the form of magnificent offerings,
Which are presented to Maitreya residing in Tushita
And also to the buddhas and bodhisattvas in all ten directions.

The blessings and inspiration of the three doors of these holy
beings
Are drawn back in the form of nectar and radiant light
That melt into the syllable and mantra at my heart,
Infusing my mind with the bliss of enlightenment.

*(Now recite the mantra as many times as possible, maintaining divine
pride and the clarity of the visualization. During the recitation, the
meditations on loving-kindness and compassion and the visualization
of purifying light and nectar can be continued.)*

Optional offerings and praise

*(At this point, if desired, you may repeat the offerings to oneself as
Maitreya and the praise above.)*

Meditation on the graduated path to enlightenment

*(At this point you may do a glance meditation on the entire graduated
path to enlightenment using short texts such as* The Foundation of All
Good Qualities, The Three Principal Aspects of the Path, Lines of
Experience *or* A Glance Meditation on All the Important Points of
the Lam-rim.[28]*—or you may select a particular point and meditate
upon its meaning.)*

After that we do the last part of the sadhana, the concluding dedication practices.[29]

I think you now understand the sadhana, so that's enough.

---

[28] See *The Joy of Compassion, Virtue and Reality* and *Illuminating the Path to Enlightenment*
respectively (all published for free distribution by the Lama Yeshe Wisdom Archive) for the
first three texts and Appendix 4 of this book for *A Glance Meditation on All the Important
Points of the Lam-rim.* They're also all on line at www.LamaYeshe.com.
[29] See Appendix 2.

11. Retreat[30]

IN THE FIRST morning session, before breakfast, do the sadhana from beginning to end. It should take about an hour and a quarter. So start off with sessions of about that length and then gradually extend them as the retreat progresses. That's the Tibetan style: start with short sessions, then, depending on how your meditation is going, make them longer. But don't spend too much time on mantra recitation; one *mala* should be enough. Your main emphasis should be on developing concentration.

In the second session, instead of starting at the very beginning of the sadhana, start with the main body of the yoga method, with meditation on shunyata, self-generation, one mala of mantra recitation and dedication. Do the rest of the sessions in the same way.

Also, I strongly recommend that you maintain silence, at least until midday. That's the way to experience strong transformation. Otherwise, if you just blah, blah, blah to each other all day, you'll simply dissipate whatever energy you've gained.

Buddhism is very simple and practical. We need to transform our body, speech and mind, and the meditations in the yoga method are set up to facilitate this transformation. We transform our flesh and blood body into the clear light nature of Maitreya's body; our utterly nonsensical speech, which is usually symptomatic of ego, into the pure energy of mantra, free of dualistic games; and our garbage thoughts into Maitreya's universal love and non-dual wisdom. These are the three things we need to do.

In between sessions, there's a break. From the Tibetan point of view, the session break is just as important as the session, if not more. After

[30] See *Becoming Vajrasattva* for detailed group and individual retreat instructions.

you've cleaned your room you don't turn around and throw dirt all over it; similarly, after you've purified yourself during the session you don't want to fill your mind with more garbage.

Therefore be mindful. During the breaks continue to recognize yourself as Maitreya, with a radiant golden body in the nature of universal love and compassion, and to see other people in the same way as well. If you can maintain this kind of awareness there's no way that superstition can arise.

Also, eat and drink mindfully, recognizing the nature of whatever you ingest as the universal love and wisdom of Maitreya—everything you eat and drink causes incredibly blissful energy to explode in your nervous system, like throwing gasoline on a fire. Every meal fills you with indescribable bliss.

The main emphasis of tantra is on the experience of satisfaction and bliss. Tantra is the path to complete psychological satisfaction. Along the way, your mind automatically becomes focused, incisive and clear.

Sleeping

You can sleep in one of two ways but first of all make sure you're comfortable. From the tantric point of view, sleeping well is good, eating well is good. So sleep very comfortably. Some people's beds are very uncomfortable; I don't see the point of that. Be comfortable. There's no use in making life harder than it already is.

When I first came to the West I was shocked by how soft the mattresses were; I couldn't lie flat. Now my students know that I need a firm bed. For me, soft beds are very uncomfortable, but I think the fashion's now changing in favor of hard beds. In the seventies, everybody wanted a soft bed.

The first way to sleep is to transform into Maitreya, lie down in the lion position[31] and go to sleep like that. Buddhism considers this a very

---

[31] Lie on your right side, cradle your head in the palm of your right hand and lay your left arm straight down your left side to your thigh. "Reclining Buddha" statues usually show him in the lion position.

profound way to sleep because it's the way Lord Buddha slept and passed away. Don't sleep flat on your back or on your stomach unless it's for medical reasons. If you die in your sleep in the wrong position it can adversely affect your rebirth because your nervous system isn't working properly. Sleeping is also part of the path to enlightenment.

You usually hear some sounds when you awaken—instead of thinking of them as ordinary, imagine that they're the sound of mantra coming from space to wake you up. When you bathe and dress, again see yourself in the clear light nature of Maitreya and offer yourself a bath and clothes. Of course, Maitreya doesn't need to wash, but we offer him a bath in order to clean our dualistic mind. When you have breakfast, again offer your food and drink to yourself as Maitreya and experience bliss as I mentioned before.

During the day, a good technique to employ whenever you're in a situation where anger is likely to arise is to emanate as Maitreya. This is an excellent way of controlling anger. If you're going into a situation where you know you're likely to get angry, first manifest strongly as Maitreya. If you do, there's no way you'll get angry.

In fact, the light of Maitreya's radiant golden body is particularly powerful in stopping the symptoms of *any* delusion because all destructive emotions arise from darkness and lack of clarity. The golden light is wisdom, which always energizes sensitivity and awareness.

The second way of sleeping goes like this. Generate yourself as Maitreya, lie in the lion position and visualize all living beings and their environments—everything in the universe—melting into light and sinking into you. Then you, Maitreya, gradually dissolve into light from your feet up, finally absorbing into the mantra and moon disc at your heart. The moon disc and mantra dissolve into the syllable HUM, the HUM dissolves from below up and disappears into non-dual wisdom, and you go to sleep in emptiness. Thus sleep again becomes the path to enlightenment. When you wake in the morning, meditate strongly on the shunyata experience and arise from it as Maitreya.

Group retreat

In the future, in my absence or that of another teacher, I think it would be good for Maitreya Institute to organize retreats on this yoga method. Personally, I also think it would be all right for people who have not had the initiation to join such retreats. Because this is Maitreya Institute we can make the exception that people can practice Maitreya without initiation. There would be much benefit from that. In Tibet we did have the system where people without initiation could join a group deity yoga retreat but not do the practice individually. Also, you have tapes of this commentary and senior students to lead the meditations, so it should be easy.

You should also organize other deity yoga retreats, such as Chenrezig and lam-rim retreats as well. The point is to try to benefit others as much as possible. Retreats are very useful in restoring people's energy and helping them become strong.

Prostrations

As long as you're healthy it's good to do strong prostrations in retreat but if you're not then it's better not to. However, we do need healthy bodies, so instead of doing nonsensical kinds of exercise it's better to do prostrations, which are very powerful. Firstly, touching the ground itself is healing, but prostrations are also very helpful psychologically, because our ego doesn't ever want to admit it's wrong. Even when we make an obvious mistake we can't accept somebody's pointing it out.

So we have to train our mind in humility and making prostrations is a way of doing so, of making space in our mind to accept things, good or bad. It's very important that we have the space in our mind to say, "Yes, you're right," when somebody says, "You made a mistake." Making mistakes is as much a part of being human as is doing the right thing. So prostrations are important.

We should also understand that when we make prostrations we're not making them to the material objects on the altar—the statues, *thangkas*, photographs and so forth—but to the universal love, compassion and understanding of non-duality of which they're a manifestation. We know how incredibly beneficial these enlightened qualities are, so we prostrate to them, not the physical atoms that represent them. Be sensible—prostrating to mere material atoms doesn't make any sense at all.

So every time we see the holy objects on the altar and bring to mind the profound qualities and achievements they symbolize—Maitreya's enlightened universal love, compassion and wisdom—we receive a great impression in our mind.

Of course, if we don't have the mad elephant characteristics of self-pity pride in our mind we don't need to make prostrations, but most of us are probably not at that level. Also, prostrations constitute an integral part of the preliminary practices,[32] so it's certain that beginners like us need to do them.

The way to practice is to do some actual meditation, like on the graduated path to enlightenment or deity yoga, then some preliminary practice to elevate the mind a little, then some more actual meditation, then some more preliminary practice and so forth. We should use all the resources at our disposal to develop our mind.

At the same time, we should not hold the fanatical view that we can't attain enlightenment without making prostrations. That's wrong, too. I'm just extolling the virtues of prostrations because I have found them to be very helpful in my life in general and in subduing my ego in particular.

---

[32] There are nine preliminary practices in the Gelug tradition: prostration, mandala offering, refuge, Vajrasattva, guru yoga, water-bowls, Samayavajra, tsa-tsas, and Vajradaka fire puja.

12. Questions and answers

Q: Is it important during retreat that there be no children around?
Lama: It depends. If they're older, like six or eight, perhaps they can go to somebody's house nearby to play, but if they're too young to be left alone like this and somebody can take care of them during the sessions, it's OK. Then during the breaks the parents can feed and play with them and give them some love. You need to be flexible.

Q: Lama, if we cannot stay for the retreat is there some way we can carry the initiation over to daily life?
Lama: Definitely. If you like, you can practice the main body of the meditation every day, but to be practical it's probably better that you focus on just one meditation technique a day. You can't cover all the techniques in one day if you're working and have other responsibilities. Do whatever your time allows. Also, it might be hard to do the whole sadhana every day; Western life can be difficult that way.

For example, if you have to go to work and don't have time to meditate in the morning, when you get home you can shower, relax and, when your mind is clean clear, practice the meditation techniques. If your mind is really busy, first meditate on your breath for a while and then go into the experience of shunyata, manifest as Maitreya and practice developing your concentration. It's better to focus on one particular practice in a session rather than try to do several, which prevents transformation.

The sadhana looks simple but it's not. I've tried here to explain its essence; to do it in detail would take more than a month. It's really profound. It contains the entire lam-rim—every type of Buddhist meditation. But although you can integrate every kind of meditation into this sadhana, what you need to focus on is putting your wisdom energy into the nuclear essence of the practice.

That's why these particular yoga meditations are so useful. If you understand the gradual, step-by-step transformational process clean clear, you know how to reach enlightenment and don't get confused. Even if you hear non-Buddhist teachings, you know how they relate; when a Christian minister talks about the Bible you come away thinking, "Wow, that helps my practice of the Maitreya yoga method." No matter what you listen to, you have the wisdom to understand where it fits into the path to enlightenment.

If you don't understand how all the teachings fit together into one coherent path, the more you read and hear, the more confused you get. Instead of producing clarity, everything you encounter simply produces more superstition. Instead of destroying delusion, the things you read and hear increase doubt and indecision and leave you with no spiritual strength or understanding of how to better yourself or others.

Therefore it's good to understand how the sadhana is set up and how all the Buddha's teachings fit into this one essential framework.

Q: Is it important to receive conscious transmission of a mantra? I'm not sure if I received the Maitreya mantra or not. Perhaps I received it unconsciously.
Lama: The mantra was given during the initiation; if you were there, you received it. But don't worry if you don't remember; experiences can be conscious or unconscious. Sometimes you can experience something in meditation that you don't recall after the session. It's like a dream. You can also have unbelievably profound experiences in a dream but when you wake up they're too subtle for you to remember. When your gross mind restarts there's no space for you to comprehend what happened when you were asleep.

Q: I have to leave halfway through the retreat. Would it be better not to start and try to do the whole thing another time?
Lama: It's better to do what you can whenever you can. Two days are

better than nothing; two days' Maitreya yoga method practice is actually very precious. The more you practice the sooner you get enlightened. That's logical, isn't it? Then, in future, according to your time, you can do the retreat alone at home or perhaps a longer group retreat somewhere else.

Retreat is an incredibly powerful way to develop and transform yourself. You can make much more progress by retreating intensively for ten days than you can by listening to teachings for a year, because in retreat you deal with things on a more organic level. Words are kind of artificial; listening to teachings can produce more confusion because words *are* confusion—it doesn't matter how many you use, they still all come from superstition. So retreat is super; very useful.

Also, the Tibetan yoga system is set up very practically. When you go into retreat you feel that there's already a system, so you don't have to ask, "What do I do now?" It's all set up as a graduated path—you can tell what level of development you're on and what you have to do next.

With respect to group retreat, even though the retreat leader might be reading the sadhana aloud and everybody else is meditating accordingly, you don't necessarily have to follow along. You can do your own Maitreya meditation. The leader is obliged to read the sadhana as written but even though you've come for group retreat, as an individual you don't necessarily have to follow. You've received the commentary and know what it's about, so you can choose whatever aspect of the practice you like and just meditate on that.

So now you're going to ask, "Why bother coming for group retreat? I might as well do it alone." But a group situation gives you energy; the more Maitreyas come, the more energy you get. Therefore it's helpful. I've done many group retreats but I didn't always do what the group did.

Q: I practice a Guru Padmasambhava sadhana and I'm wondering if it's possible to combine it with Maitreya practice, especially the sleep yoga?
Lama: That's simple. The qualities of Guru Padmasambhava are those of Maitreya and the qualities of Maitreya are those of Guru Padmasambhava, so what's the problem?

Q: The technical visualizations are a little different. How can I combine them?

Lama: I'm not sure how you want to combine them; there are hundreds of ways you could. Still, I think the best way would be to practice one in the morning and the other in the evening because they emphasize different energies. Padmasambhava practice is especially useful for guru yoga.

Q: My question is mainly in relation to going to sleep because each practice has a different visualization for doing that.

Lama: Then you can choose whichever you like according to what you think you need but if you really want to combine them, perhaps you can first do Guru Padmasambhava meditation: he sinks into you, you become one with Guru Padmasambhava, your body becomes light and you disappear into the experience of shunyata. When you come out of that, emerge as Maitreya. That would be an excellent way to combine the two practices.

Q: Can you tell us something about the meaning of the Maitreya mantra?

Lama: To really explain it would take more than a month but I can briefly mention the meaning of the short mantra, OM AH MAITRI SARVA SIDDHI HUM.

+ OM is the unity of the pure, or divine, qualities of Maitreya's holy body, speech and mind. What do I mean by unity? At present, our body, speech and mind are split. Our body functions differently from our speech and mind, our speech functions differently from our body and mind and our mind functions differently from our body and speech, but when we attain a certain level of realization, all three function as one. That's why developing unity is one of the things we practice.
+ AH is Maitreya Buddha's pure speech.
+ MAITRI is Sanskrit for universal love and compassion.
+ SARVA means all; SIDDHI means realizations; together they mean all realizations.

✦ HUM means universal wisdom; the omniscient wisdom that understands universal reality.

But this is just a literal explanation. When you explain the actual meaning of a mantra you have to go beyond the literal, so there are many ways of explaining it. If I were to really explain the meaning of OM MANI PADME HUM, for example, it would take me a year.

Conclusion

Well, I think that's all we have time for. Buddhism believes that my consciousness and yours can unite in the ocean of universal conscious energy, so that's the beauty of our having come together here. Even though we have different personalities, different noses, different mouths, different ears, and different nationalities, we have still somehow come together and been able to communicate with each other. That really signifies universal love, the meaning of Maitreya. In the true sense of the word I think we *are* Maitreya. So we're very lucky and I'm grateful for this opportunity. Thank you for having listened to my garbage words and I would especially like to thank all the Maitreya Institute people who worked so hard to organize this event. I will dedicate the energy you have expended for you to grow in the universal love and compassion of Maitreya. Thank you so much.

Finally, let's dedicate whatever experience we've had generating love and compassion and touching reality to the benefit of all beings in the universe—through this energy, may they attain the qualities of Maitreya.

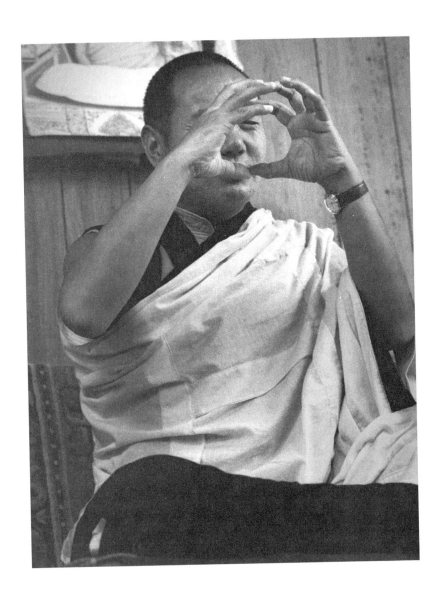

Appendix 1

AN EXPLANATION OF THE SHUNYATA MANTRA
AND A MEDITATION ON EMPTINESS

THE MAIN BODY of the yoga meditation begins with the shunyata mantra, OM SVABHAVA SHUDDHO SARVA DHARMA SVABHAVA SHUDDHO HAM.

First, it's significant that the words of this mantra are the original Sanskrit—just hearing or reciting them imparts great blessings.

Also, this mantra contains a profound explanation of the pure, fundamental nature of both human beings and all other existent phenomena. It means that everything is spontaneously pure—not relatively, of course, but in the absolute sense. From the absolute point of view, the fundamental quality of human beings and the nature of all things is purity.

We need to understand what the mantra means by "nature," or "natural." Much of the time we are unnatural; we go against our nature. Our ego tries to be clever and intelligent; it's always dreaming up ways to generate hatred, anger and desire, but that's bad, negative intelligence. It creates an artificial self and then believes that this artificial self is the real me: "This is me; look how beautiful I am." We present an artificial emanation to ourselves, believe that this false image is real, and then present ourselves to others in that way.

As long as we're on this kind of psychological ego trip we can never be natural. In order to touch our fundamental nature we have to go beyond our false self. When we do, we touch purity.

Thus the shunyata mantra also shows that the self-pity wrong conception that constantly repeats in our mind—"I'm hopeless, I'm impure, I'm a bad person, I'm evil, I can't do anything, I can't help myself, I can't help others"—is completely deluded and an unnatural way to think. In other words, Lord Buddha's philosophy and psychology teach us that we should not believe that we are totally negative or sinful by nature. That's absolutely incorrect. Our fundamental nature is pure. The artificial cloud projected by our ego is not our nature; it's just something fabricated by our intellectual ego. Therefore, we should disregard this wrong view and just be natural, as we are.

Let me give you an example of how we're not natural. Look at how people have changed through the history of human evolution. Women have changed their image; men have changed the way they work. Have you noticed? I have. I don't look at the world from only the religious point of view; I observe human history, too. This kind of change explains the generation gap: old people don't understand the way young people act. They look at them and think, "What on earth is *that*?" Young people look at the elderly and think they're out of touch. They see their peers acting and dressing in a certain way, believe that that's the best way to be, and adopt a new kind of emanation. But it's completely artificial, not at all natural. Therefore, through understanding the fundamental nature of the human being, we should try to be natural.

The shunyata mantra shows the positive reality of what a human is. Why should we have only a negative self-image? That's just ego. And that's why Buddhism never has anything good to say about the ego. From our point of view, the ego is always bad because all it brings is suffering. And that's why we practice meditation—it's the way we transcend artificial thought, gain peaceful tranquility and touch our fundamental reality.

Reciting the shunyata mantra helps us cut the conceptions that lead us to misery, such as ideas of permanence and the inherent existence of the self. Such conceptions *should* be cut. If they are not completely eradicated they just build up; they diminish today and tomorrow recur. We have no control. We suppress something here, it comes out there; we suppress something there, it comes out here. Sublimating problems is no solution.

Anyway, whether or not you recite the shunyata mantra, the important thing to understand is that the self-pity image of yourself to which you cling does not exist. I could easily explain this in a detailed, philosophical way but the simple approach is to look at how you hold yourself today—"I am that-this"—and compare that with how you held yourself last year. Do you hold yourself the same way or has your self-conception changed? It's actually very difficult for that to change—we always feel that the "me" of today is exactly the same as the "me" of last year. But of course, that's wrong, both relatively and absolutely.

First of all, things are constantly changing in the shortest fraction of a second. There's no way that the Mr. Jones of today can be exactly the same as the Mr. Jones of yesterday. It's just not possible. And when you clearly see the way in which you hold a permanent self-image, all you can do is laugh at yourself. It's just so nonsensical. You believe that you're the same person you were ten years ago. That's what Lord Buddha meant when he said that we're deluded, deluded, deluded!

Deluded means holding and hanging on to nonsensical conceptions and hallucinated projections of ourselves and as long as we don't eradicate this cause of all problems, we're not doing a good job. We can meditate for twenty or thirty years but if we don't touch the root of problems, if we don't shake our ego, if all we do is make it more beautiful and solid, we're not doing a good job at all.

What we need to do is to shake our samsara, the root of ego, the way our ego conception holds things. When we shake the Mt. Meru of our ego, our entire samsaric mandala collapses. That's a real earthquake.

Lord Buddha's teaching on universal reality is so profound. It shows us the best way to be healthy by shattering all our concepts and illusions. He said, "Even if you hold concepts of me, the Buddha, you're still trapped in samsara."

The so-called religious practitioners of today are going to run to their guru saying, "You're a fantastic guru, I love you; please love me." They're going to want their self-existent guru to love their self-existent selves. That's their ego at work. If people had run up to the Buddha like that he'd have told them to get lost. That's beautiful. Lord Buddha didn't want people to be hung up grasping at anything, much less him and his doctrine. He said that such people were foolish; that that was no way to be healthy. He said even if we're attached to the bodhisattva path, the six perfections, the tantric path—any Buddhist philosophy—we're trapped.

It's very simple. Lord Buddha made no exceptions. He said that we should grasp at neither samsaric nor religious phenomena, not even Buddhist philosophy. His aim was universal health.

We also find that many gurus are attached to their disciples and want their disciples to be attached to them. That's totally wrong, too. Gurus should not be attached to their disciples; disciples should not be attached to their guru. True spiritual practitioners should not be attached to any person, doctrine or philosophy. It's unhealthy. The Buddha taught so that we might also become buddha: healthy, eternally happy and free of all concepts, misery, doctrine and bondage. That's all he wanted.

Therefore we have to recognize the falsity of the conception of the permanent, concrete self of last year that we're clinging to right now and break it down; we have to see how our ego-grasping creates an atmosphere of ignorance within which we then grasp at sense pleasures, which tantalize and trick us by their dancing in the dark.

This shunyata mantra is most profound: "All existent phenomena in the universe and I are of one reality." At the moment, our ego divides us from other phenomena. It says, "You are this, this, this; I am that, that, that." It keeps us from getting close to even our loved ones. We spend our whole life with another person but never get really close because of the games our ego plays. Our ego prevents us from understanding one another.

The mantra finishes with, "That is me," HAM. "All existent phenomena in the universe and I are of one reality and that is me; I am that." This signifies divine pride. Through experiencing shunyata we experience a kind of unity of self and other, like pouring milk into milk. When you mix two lots of milk they become indistinguishable from one another. That is the beauty of the nature of shunyata—understanding, experiencing or realizing it makes our dualistic mind vanish. Dual means two; relatively speaking, you and I are dual. But from the ultimate point of view, when I realize my universal nature and yours, we become indistinguishable.

People talk about racism: it's a bad thing, we should do away with it; many people have been killed as a result of racism. From the Buddhist point of view, without destroying the dualistic ego there's no way to eliminate racism; it's too deeply rooted within. So until we discover the reality of universal unity, any talk of racism disappearing is a joke. It's just not possible.

However, Lord Buddha gave precise, practical teachings on overcoming duality that we can implement in our everyday life. That's the beauty of being human; that's why from the Buddhist point of view, humans are beautiful. In the relative world we can practice charity and so forth but we can also transcend the relative world; we're capable of both functioning in the relative world and going beyond it into the absolute.

Experiencing emptiness

From the practical point of view, tantric techniques help us gain direct experience of shunyata. The usual way to do this is to first visualize the deity that you are practicing—Maitreya, for example—in space in front of you, seeing this deity as your guru, a buddha or a bodhisattva, depending upon your level of understanding. A laser-like beam of radiant white light emanates from Maitreya's heart and shoots into your heart, transforming all the energy of the self-pity image you have of yourself into radiant white light. This white light image of yourself then gradually dissolves, becoming smaller and smaller until it completely disappears into the space of non-duality. Then, with complete awareness, you concentrate single-pointedly on that.

This technique for experiencing emptiness epitomizes the tantric approach. Lord Buddha taught tantra so that we could not only understand emptiness intellectually but also to experience it directly.

If you want to practice this technique right now, do it as follows. First, close your eyes. We meditate with our eyes closed because, from the Buddhist point of view, sense perception is no good—the moment we open our eyes we're assailed by dualistic impressions. So close your eyes and visualize Maitreya in the space in front of you. As if magnetically attracted, a laser beam of radiant white light shoots out of his heart into yours, instantly burning up your entire concrete self-image. This nuclear energy transforms your body into radiant white light. It gets smaller and smaller, dissolves into atoms, neutrons…and completely disappears into selflessness. Remain in this state, fully aware, and just experience it without any intellectualization; just let go.

[Meditation]

Your normal, ego-conceived self-image disappears. Think strongly that it has completely gone. Let go.

[Meditation]

Think, "My self-pity image of myself is universal reality." Feel this, fully aware; let go without intellectualization.

[Meditation]

Think, "In the great universal reality of emptiness there's no form, no color, no substantial physical energy."

[Meditation]

"The view and experience of non-duality is great peace. This is the experience of enlightenment."

[Meditation]

Appendix 2

THE SADHANA OF BUDDHA MAITREYA

THE PRELIMINARY PRACTICES

Taking refuge

(From a state of deep faith visualize the assembly of enlightened beings and take refuge while reciting the following:)

I and all other mother sentient beings
Equal in number to the vastness of space
From this moment until we reach enlightenment
Take heartfelt refuge in the three Rare and Precious Gems
And especially in Maitreya Buddha. (x3)

Taking refuge and generating bodhicitta

I go for refuge until I am enlightened
To the Buddha, the Dharma and the Supreme Assembly.
By my practice of giving and other perfections,
May I become a buddha to benefit all sentient beings. (x3)

The four immeasurables

(a) Immeasurable equanimity

How wonderful it would be if all sentient beings
Were to abide in equanimity,
Free from hatred and attachment,

Not holding some close and others distant.
May they abide in equanimity;
I myself will cause them to abide in equanimity;
Please, guru-deity, bless me to be able to do this.

(While reciting this and the three following prayers, first visualize white puri-fying light coming from the objects of refuge, cleansing you of all obstacles that interfere with the generation of each immeasurable thought; then visualize golden yellow light coming from the objects of refuge, granting you the full realization of each thought.)

(b) Immeasurable love

How wonderful it would be if all sentient beings
Had happiness and the causes of happiness.
May they have happiness and its causes;
I myself will cause them to have happiness and its causes;
Please, guru-deity, bless me to be able to do this.

(c) Immeasurable compassion

How wonderful it would be if all sentient beings
Were free from suffering and the causes of suffering.
May they be free from suffering and its causes;
I myself will cause them to be free from suffering and its causes;
Please, guru-deity, bless me to be able to do this.

(d) Immeasurable joy

How wonderful it would be if all sentient beings
Were never separated from the happiness of higher rebirth and liberation.
May they never be separated from these;
I myself will cause them never to be separated from these;
Please, guru-deity, bless me to be able to do this.

Generating special bodhicitta

(Recite and think deeply about the following:)

For the sake of all mother sentient beings
I shall quickly, quickly, in this very life,
Attain the state of enlightenment.
Therefore, I shall now practice
The profound yogic method of Buddha Maitreya.

THE MAIN BODY

Emptiness meditation

OM SVABHAVA SHUDDHA SARVA DHARMA SVABHAVA SHUDDHO HAM

I and all universally existent phenomena are recognized as non-duality.

(While reciting this mantra, contemplate on the non-dual nature of all phenomena, including yourself. Meditate upon the emptiness of inherent existence; then from the space of this emptiness arise as follows:)

Emergence from emptiness

In the empty space of non-duality
Appear eight mighty snow lions
Supporting a precious jeweled throne
Upon which rests a lotus and moon disc.
And upon this vast, white moon disc
My mind manifests as a syllable HUM,[33]
Brilliant golden light, the size of a sesame seed.

[33] Or you can visualize the seed syllable of Maitreya, MEM.

(Let your mind sink into this syllable completely and try to contemplate without differentiation of subject and object. You are this golden syllable HUM.)

Accomplishing the two purposes

From this syllable
Radiant light shines out in all ten directions
Making offerings of exquisite beauty to all buddhas and bodhisattvas
And then purifying the negative energy of all sentient beings,
Leading them to the state of enlightenment.
Once these two purposes have been accomplished
This light dissolves back into my mind.

Self-generation

Instantly
I become Maitreya Buddha,
With a clear light body, golden in color,
With one face and two arms.
My two hands are poised at my heart
In the mudra of turning the wheel of Dharma.
In each hand I hold the stem of a lotus;
Upon the right is a wheel; upon the left is a vase.
My black hair is pulled back and tied in a knot
And my head is crowned with a stupa of enlightenment.
My face wears a smiling, peaceful expression
And my body is adorned with the eighty qualities
And thirty-two marks of magnificence.
Precious ornaments decorate my body
And I emanate an aura of five-colored light
As I am seated in the majestic position
With my feet planted firmly upon the ground.
Three syllables adorn my body:

A white OM at my crown,
A red AH at my throat
And a blue HUM at my heart.

Invocation of the wisdom beings

From the blue HUM at my heart,
Much brilliant blue light radiates out to Tushita,
Invoking the wisdom beings in the form of Maitreya,
Who come back with the light and melt into me.

(Generate the strong divine pride that you have actually become Maitreya Buddha and visualize yourself vividly as having a brilliant form made of clear light, as transparent as crystal.)

Offerings to oneself as Maitreya

(a) Removing interferences

(Recite the following mantra while visualizing that all impure energies— particularly those deriving from the mistaken view of inherent existence—are chased away from the objects of offering:)

OM VAJRA AMRITA KUNDALI HANA HANA HUM PHAT

(b) Dissolution into emptiness

OM SVABHAVA SHUDDHA SARVA DHARMA SVABHAVA SHUDDHO HAM
Everything becomes empty

(c) Transformation and blessing

All the offerings are recognized as non-duality,
Yet manifesting in the form of the individual offerings

And functioning to elicit the experience of bliss,
As objects to be enjoyed by all the six senses.

(The elaborate visualization can be done as follows. The eight objects of offering dissolve into emptiness, from which the eight syllables OM *appear. These transform into offering bowls each containing the syllable* HUM. *The* HUMs *dissolve into light and transform into the individual objects of offering. Then visualize that above each offering bowl are the syllables* OM, AH *and* HUM *in ascending order. Recite the following eight blessing mantras. As you recite* OM, *white light radiates from the syllable above the first offering into the ten directions of space and draws the enlightened quality of the holy body of all buddhas and bodhisattvas back into the* OM, *which then sinks into the offering bowl. In a similar fashion, red light from the* AH *and blue from the* HUM *draw back the enlightened qualities of the speech and mind of these holy beings. In this way all eight offerings are transformed and blessed.)*

OM ARGHAM AH HUM
OM PADYAM AH HUM
OM PUSHPE AH HUM
OM DHUPE AH HUM
OM ALOKE AH HUM
OM GANDE AH HUM
OM NAIVIDYA AH HUM
OM SHAPTA AH HUM

(d) Presentation of the offerings

(While reciting the following offering mantras and performing the appropriate mudras, visualize offering goddesses emanating from your heart, presenting the offerings to yourself as Maitreya Buddha and then dissolving back into your heart.)

OM ARYA ARGHAM PRATICCHA HUM SVAHA[34]

OM ARYA PADYAM PRATICCHA HUM SVAHA

OM ARYA PUSHPE PRATICCHA HUM SVAHA

OM ARYA DHUPE PRATICCHA HUM SVAHA

OM ARYA ALOKE PRATICCHA HUM SVAHA

OM ARYA GANDE PRATICCHA HUM SVAHA

OM ARYA NAIVIDYA PRATICCHA HUM SVAHA

OM ARYA SHAPTA PRATICCHA HUM SVAHA

Praise

(Thinking deeply about the excellent qualities of Maitreya Buddha, recite the following prayer:)

I pay homage and offer praise to Maitreya Buddha
Who, by accomplishing the meditation of loving-kindness,
Has conquered all enemies and harm: the negative forces of Mara,
And cares for all mother sentient beings with great compassion.

Recitation of the mantra

(With strong concentration visualize the following as clearly as possible:)

At my heart is a moon disc
Upon which rests the golden syllable HUM [35]
Surrounded by the glowing letters of the mantra:
OM AH MAITRI SARVA SIDDHI HUM.

From these much brilliant light radiates in all ten directions
Filling the entire universe and purifying all negative energy
—Just as the rays of the sun instantly eliminate darkness—
And leading all beings to the state of Maitreya Buddha.

[34] Or OM ARYA MAITREYA ARGHAM PRATICCHA HUM SVAHA…etc.
[35] Or MEM.

Again light radiates forth in the form of magnificent offerings,
Which are presented to Maitreya, residing in Tushita,
And also to the buddhas and bodhisattvas in all ten directions.

The blessings and inspiration of the three doors of these holy beings
Are drawn back in the form of nectar and radiant light
That melt into the syllable and mantra at my heart,
Infusing my mind with the bliss of enlightenment.

(Now recite the mantra as many times as possible, maintaining divine pride and the clarity of the visualization. During the recitation, the meditations on loving-kindness and compassion and the visualization of purifying light and nectar can be continued.)

Optional offerings and praise

(At this point, if desired, you may repeat the offerings to oneself as Maitreya and the praise above.)

Meditation on the graduated path to enlightenment

(At this point you may do a glance meditation on the entire graduated path to enlightenment—using short texts such as The Foundation of All Good Qualities, The Three Principal Aspects of the Path, Lines of Experience *or* A Glance Meditation on All the Important Points of the Lam-rim[36]—*or you may select a particular point and meditate upon its meaning.)*

---

[36] See Appendix 4.

CONCLUSION

Dedication

(By means of the following prayers, dedicate whatever positive energy has been generated by this meditation to the complete enlightenment of all mother sentient beings:)

Due to the merits of these virtuous actions
May I quickly attain the state of Buddha Maitreya
And lead all living beings, without exception,
Into his enlightened state.

May the supreme jewel bodhicitta
That has not arisen, arise and grow;
And may that which has arisen not diminish
But increase more and more.

Colophon: This sadhana was prepared from teachings given by Lama Thubten Yeshe at Tushita Retreat Centre Dharamsala, India in March, 1981, in response to requests made by members of Maitreya Institute, Netherlands. It was first edited by Jonathan Landaw and re-edited for this book by Nicholas Ribush. May all beings be happy!

Appendix 3

THE MANTRA OF MAITREYA BUDDHA'S PROMISE
(*Arya-Maitrina-pratijna-nama-dharani*)

The root mantra

NAMO RATNA TRAYAYA
Homage to the Three Jewels

NAMO BHAGAVATE SHAKYAMUNIYE TATHAGATAYA ARHATE SAMYAK SAM
BUDDHAYA
*Homage to the Lord Shakyamuni, Tathagata, Arhat, Completely Perfect
Buddha*

TADYATHA: OM AJITE AJITE APARAJITE
As follows: Om Invincible, Invincible, Unconquered

AJITAN CHAYA HARA HARA
Conquer the Unconquered, take, take [it]

MAITRI AVALOKITE KARA KARA
You Who Look Down with Friendliness, act, act

MAHA SAMAYA SIDDHI BHARA BHARA
Bring, bring the fulfillment of your great pledge

MAHA BODHI MÄNDA VIJA
Shake the seat of great awakening

MARA MARA ATMAKAM SAMAYA
Remember, remember [your] pledge for us

BODHI BODHI MAHA BODHI SVAHA
Awakening, awakening, great awakening, svaha

The heart mantra

OM MOHI MOHI MAHA MOHI SVAHA
Om fascinating, fascinating, greatly fascinating, svaha

The close heart mantra

OM MUNI MUNI MARA SVAHA
Om sage, sage, remember, svaha

Colophon: From Shakyamuni Puja: Worshipping the Buddha, *Appendix 2, translated and edited by Martin Willson. London: Wisdom Publications, 1988. Phonetics changed to accord with the version in FPMT's revised and expanded edition of* Lama Chöpa, *2004, page 99.*

Appendix 4

A Glance Meditation on
All the Important Points of the Lam-rim

Nature that embodies all the buddhas,
Source of all the pure transmission and realization Dharma,
Principal amongst all the arya Sangha:
I take refuge in all magnificent pure gurus.

Please bless my mind to become Dharma,
That Dharma to become the path,
And that path to be free of all hindrances.
Until I achieve enlightenment, may I,
Just like the bodhisattvas, Shönnu Norsang and Taktungu,[37]
Practice pure devotion to my guru in thought and action,
See all the actions of my guru as excellent,
And fulfill whatever he advises.
Please bless me with the potential to accomplish this.
(This is relying on the spiritual friend.)

Knowing that this highly meaningful perfect human rebirth
Is difficult to obtain and easily lost,
Realizing the profundity of cause and effect
And the unbearable sufferings of the lower realms,
From my heart I take refuge in the Three Precious Sublime Ones,

[37] Respectively, Young Sudhana in the *Flower Ornament Scripture* (*Avatamsaka Sutra*) and Sadaprarudita (Bodhisattva Always Crying) in the *Perfection of Wisdom in Eight Thousand Lines* (*Astasahasrika Prajnaparamita Sutra*), classic examples of how to practice guru devotion.

Abandon negativity, and practice virtue in accordance with the
    Dharma.
Please bless me with the potential to accomplish this.
(This is the path of the being of lower capacity.)

In dependence on this, I am able to attain
Only the higher rebirths of humans and gods.
Not having abandoned afflictions,
I have to experience uninterrupted, limitless cyclic existence.
By contemplating well how cyclic existence works,
May I train day and night in the principal path
Of the three precious higher trainings—
The means of attaining liberation.
Please bless me with the potential to always train like this.
(This is the path of the being of middle capacity.)

In dependence on this, I am able to attain only self-liberation.
As there is not one sentient being in all the six realms
Who has not been my mother or father,
I will turn away from this lower happiness
And generate the wish to fulfill their ultimate purposes.
By contemplating the path of equalizing and exchanging self
    for others,
I will generate the precious bodhicitta
And engage in the bodhisattvas' actions of the six perfections.
Please bless me with the potential to train in this way.
(This is the common path of the being of higher capacity.)

Having trained like this in the common path,
I myself will not have aversion to experiencing
The sufferings of cyclic existence for a long time,
But by the force of extraordinary unbearable compassion for sentient
    beings,
May I enter the quick path of the Vajrayana.
By observing purely my vows and pledges even at the cost of my life,

May I quickly attain the unified state of Vajradhara
In one brief lifetime of this degenerate age.
Please bless me with the potential to attain this.
(This is the secret mantra vajra vehicle of the being of highest capacity.)

Colophon: This glance meditation on the lam-rim was composed by Vajra-dhara Losang Jinpa. Translated by Ven. Thubten Dekyong; lightly edited by Maureen O'Malley and Ven. Ailsa Cameron; lightly polished for distribu-tion at the 1999 Vajrasattva retreat, Land of Medicine Buddha, by Ven. Ailsa Cameron, Ven. Constance Miller and Nicholas Ribush, April 1999.

Appendix 5

What is Buddhism? Public lecture, Los Angeles, USA, 28 June 1975. Archive number 206001.

The Purpose of Meditation. Public lecture, Los Angeles, USA, 28 June 1975. Archive number 206002.

Compassion and Emptiness. Public lecture, Deer Park Buddhist Center, Madison, Wisconsin, USA, 24 August 1975. Archive number 348001.

The Yoga Method of Buddha Maitreya. Maitreya Institute, Bruchem, Holland, September 1981. Archive number 354001.

Appendix 1: From Avalokiteshvara commentary, Tushita Mahayana Meditation Center, New Delhi, 6 November 1981. Archive number 649002.

Glossary

(Skt = Sanskrit; Tib = Tibetan)
If the word you are looking for is not here, please check the online glossary at
www.LamaYeshe.com.

affliction. See *delusion.*

aggregates (Skt: skandha). The five psycho-physical constituents that make up most sentient beings: form, feeling, discriminative awareness, conditioning (compositional) factors and consciousness.

anger. A coarse mind that sees its object as repugnant and whose function is destructive; one of the six principal delusions and three poisonous minds. (Also referred to as hatred or aversion.)

arhat (Skt). Literally, foe destroyer. A person who has destroyed his or her inner enemy, the delusions, and attained liberation from cyclic existence.

arya (Skt; Tib: phag-pa). Literally, noble. One who has realized the wisdom of emptiness.

Asanga, Arya. The Indian Buddhist philosopher who was born about nine hundred years after the death of Shakyamuni Buddha and founded the Cittamatra School of Buddhist philosophy

attachment. A deluded mind that sees its object as attractive and sinks into and cannot separate from it; one of the six principal delusions and three poisonous minds.

bodhicitta (Skt). The altruistic determination to reach enlightenment for the sole purpose of enlightening all sentient beings.

bodhisattva (Skt). Someone whose spiritual practice is directed towards the achievement of enlightenment. One who possesses the compassionate motivation of bodhicitta.

buddha (Skt). A fully enlightened being. One who has removed all obscurations veiling the mind and has developed all good qualities to perfection. The first of the Three Jewels of Refuge. See also *enlightenment, Shakyamuni Buddha.*

Buddhadharma (Skt). The teachings of the Buddha. See also *Dharma.*

buddha-nature. The clear light nature of mind possessed by all sentient beings; the potential for all sentient beings to become enlightened by removing the two obscurations: to liberation and omniscience.

Buddhism. See *Dharma.*

Buddhist. One who has taken refuge in the Three Jewels of Refuge— Buddha, Dharma and Sangha—and who accepts the philosophical world view of the "four seals": that all conditioned things are impermanent, all conditioned things are dissatisfactory in nature, all phenomena are empty and nirvana is true peace.

Chandrakirti (Skt). The sixth century A.D. Indian Buddhist philosopher who wrote commentaries on Nagarjuna's philosophy. His best known work is *A Guide to the Middle Way (Madhyamakavatara).*

channels (Skt: nadi). A constituent of the vajra body through which energy winds and drops flow. The central, right, and left are the major channels; the channels total 72,000 in all.

Chenrezig (Tib; Skt: Avalokiteshvara). The Buddha of Compassion, of whom His Holiness the Dalai Lama is a manifestation. His mantra is OM MANI PADME HUM. A meditational deity.

clear appearance. The clear, vivid appearance of oneself as a meditational deity when practicing a tantric sadhana.

compassion (Skt: karuna). The sincere wish that others to be separated from their mental and physical suffering and the feeling that their freedom from suffering is more important than one's own. A prerequisite for the development of bodhicitta.

consciousness. See *mind.*

cyclic existence (Skt: samsara; Tib: khor-wa). The six realms of conditioned existence, three lower—hell, hungry ghost *(Skt: preta)* and animal—and three upper—human, demigod *(Skt: asura)* and god *(Skt: sura)*. It is the beginningless, recurring cycle of death and rebirth under the control of delusion and karma and fraught with suffering. It also refers to the contaminated aggregates of a sentient being.

daka (Skt; Tib: kha-dro). Literally, a "sky-goer." A male being who helps arouse blissful energy in a qualified tantric practitioner.

dakini (Skt; Tib: kha-dro-ma). Literally, a "female sky-goer." A female being who helps arouse blissful energy in a qualified tantric practitioner.

deity. A manifestation of the enlightened mind usually emphasizing a certain quality, such as compassion, wisdom, power and so forth, with which a practitioner identifies when practicing a tantric sadhana.

delusion (Skt: klesha). An obscuration covering the essentially pure nature of mind, being thereby responsible for suffering and dissatisfaction. There are six principal and twenty secondary delusions; the main delusion is ignorance, out of which grow desirous attachment, hatred, jealousy and all the others.

dharani. A Sanskrit phrase similar to a mantra.

Dharma (Skt). Spiritual teachings, particularly those of Shakyamuni Buddha. Literally, that which holds one back from suffering. The second of the Three Jewels of Refuge.

dharmakaya (Skt). The "buddha-body of reality." The omniscient mind of a fully enlightened being, which, free of all coverings, remains meditatively absorbed in the direct perception of emptiness while simultaneously cognizing all phenomena. The result of the complete and perfect accumulation of wisdom. One of the holy bodies of a buddha (see also *nirmanakaya, rupakaya* and *sambhogakaya*).

divine pride. The strong conviction that one has achieved the state of a particular meditational deity when practicing a tantric sadhana.

dualistic view. The ignorant view characteristic of the unenlightened mind in which all things are falsely conceived to have concrete self-existence. To such a view, the appearance of an object is mixed with the false image of its being independent or self-existent, thereby leading to further dualistic views concerning subject and object, self and other, this and that and so forth.

ego. The wrong conception that "I am self-existent"; the self-existent I. The view of the self held by a mind that has not realized emptiness.

emptiness (Skt: shunyata). The absence of all false ideas about how things exist; specifically, the lack of the apparent independent, self-existence of phenomena.

enlightenment (Skt: bodhi). Full awakening; buddhahood. The ultimate goal of Buddhist practice, attained when all limitations have been removed from the mind and one's positive potential has been completely and perfectly realized. It is a state characterized by infinite compassion, wisdom and skill.

equilibrium. Absence of the usual discrimination of sentient beings into friend, enemy and stranger, deriving from the realization that all sentient beings are equal in wanting happiness and not wanting suffering and that since beginningless time, all beings have been all things to each other. An impartial mind that serves as the basis for the development of great love, great compassion and bodhicitta.

four noble truths. The subject of Buddha's first turning of the wheel of Dharma. The truths of suffering, the origin of suffering, the cessation of suffering, and the path to the cessation of suffering, as seen by an *arya*.

Gelug (Tib). The Virtuous Order. The order of Tibetan Buddhism founded by Lama Tsongkhapa and his disciples in the early fifteenth century.

Great Vehicle. See *Mahayana.*

guru. See *lama.*

highest yoga tantra (Skt: anuttara-yoga tantra). The fourth and supreme division of tantric practice, consisting of the generation and completion stages. Through this practice, one can attain full enlightenment within one lifetime.

Hinayana (Skt). Literally, Small, or Lesser, Vehicle. It is one of the two general divisions of Buddhism. Hinayana practitioners' motivation for following the Dharma path is principally their intense wish for personal liberation from conditioned existence, or samsara. Two types of Hinayana practitioner are identified: hearers and solitary realizers. Cf. *Mahayana.*

ignorance (Skt: avidya; Tib: ma-rig-pa). Literally, "not seeing" that which exists, or the way in which things exist. There are basically two kinds, ignorance of karma and ignorance of ultimate truth. The fundamental delusion from which all others spring. The first of the twelve links of dependent arising.

impermanence (Tib: mi-tag-pa). The gross and subtle levels of the transience of phenomena. The moment things and events come into existence, their disintegration has already begun.

inherent (or intrinsic) existence. What phenomena are empty of; the object of negation, or refutation. To ignorance, phenomena appear to exist independently, in and of themselves, to exist inherently. Cf. *emptiness.*

initiation. Transmission received from a tantric master allowing a disciple to engage in the practices of a particular meditational deity. It is also referred to as an empowerment

inner fire (Tib: tum-mo). The energy residing at the navel chakra, aroused during the completion stage of highest yoga tantra and used to bring the energy winds into the central channel. It is also called inner or psychic heat.

insight meditation (Pali: vipassana). The principal meditation taught in the Theravada tradition. It is based on the Buddha's teachings on the four foundations of mindfulness. It is sometimes called mindfulness meditation. In the Mahayana, *vipashyana (Skt)* has a different connotation, where it means investigation of and familiarization with the actual way in which things exist and is used to develop the wisdom of emptiness.

karma (Skt; Tib: lä). Action; the working of cause and effect, whereby positive actions produce happiness and negative actions produce suffering.

lama (Tib; Skt: guru). A spiritual guide or teacher. One who shows a disciple the path to liberation and enlightenment. Literally, heavy—heavy with knowledge of Dharma.

lam-rim (Tib). The graduated path. A presentation of Shakyamuni Buddha's teachings in a form suitable for the step-by-step training of a disciple. The lam-rim was first formulated by the great India teacher Atisha (Dipamkara Shrijnana, 982–1055) when he came to Tibet in 1042. See also *three principal paths*.

Lesser Vehicle. See *Hinayana*.

liberation (Skt: nirvana; Tib: thar-pa). The state of complete liberation from samsara; the goal of a practitioner seeking his or her own freedom from suffering (see also *Hinayana*). "Lower nirvana" is used to refer to this state of self-liberation, while "higher nirvana" refers to the supreme attainment of the full enlightenment of buddhahood (see also *Mahayana*).

Lord Buddha. See *Shakyamuni Buddha*.

love. The sincere wish that others be happy and the feeling that their happiness is more important than one's own; opposite in nature from attachment.

Mahayana (Skt). Literally, Great Vehicle. It is one of the two general divisions of Buddhism. Mahayana practitioners' motivation for following the Dharma path is principally their intense wish that all mother sentient beings be liberated from conditioned existence, or samsara, and attain the full enlightenment of buddhahood. The Mahayana has two divisions, Paramitayana (Sutrayana) and Vajrayana (Tantrayana, Mantrayana). Cf. *Hinayana*.

maha-anuttara (Skt). Also called anuttara. See four classes of tantra and highest yoga tantra. It is divided into generation and completion stages.

Maitreya (Skt; Tib: Jam-pa). After Shakyamuni Buddha, the next (fifth) of the thousand buddhas of this fortunate eon to descend to turn the wheel of Dharma. Presently residing in the pure land of Tushita (Ganden). Recipient of the method lineage of Shakyamuni Buddha's teachings, which, in a mystical transmission, he passed on to *Arya Asanga*.

mala (Skt). Rosary.

mandala (Skt; Tib: khyil- khor). A circular diagram symbolic of the entire universe. The abode of a meditational deity.

mantra (Skt). Literally, mind protection. Mantras are Sanskrit syllables usually recited in conjunction with the practice of a particular meditational deity that embody the qualities of that deity.

Mara (Skt). Personification of the delusions that distract us from Dharma practice; what Buddhists might call the "devil"; what Shakyamuni Buddha overcame under the bodhi tree as he strove for enlightenment.

meditation. Familiarization of the mind with appropriate objects. Technically, there are two types of meditation: analytical and placement, or concentrative.

merit. Positive imprints left on the mind by virtuous, or Dharma, actions. The principal cause of happiness.

Milarepa. A great Tibetan yogi (1052–1135); one of the founders of the Kagyu school of Tibetan Buddhism. Famed for his exemplary relationship with his teacher, Marpa, his amazing asceticism and his songs of realization, Milarepa is one of the legendary figures in the history of Tibet.

mind (Skt: citta; Tib: sem). Synonymous with consciousness *(Skt: vijnana; Tib: nam-she)* and sentience *(Skt: manas; Tib: yi).* Defined as that which is "clear and knowing"; a formless entity that has the ability to perceive objects. Mind is divided into six primary consciousnesses and fifty-one mental factors.

mind training (Tib: lo-jong). A genre of teaching that explains how to transform the mind from self-cherishing to cherishing others, eventually leading to the development of bodhicitta (see also *tong-len*).

nadi. See channels.

Nagarjuna (Skt). The second century A.D. Indian Buddhist philosopher who propounded the Madhyamaka philosophy of emptiness.

nirmanakaya (Skt). The "buddha body of perfect emanation", in which a fully enlightened being appears in order to benefit ordinary beings. See also *dharmakaya, rupakaya* and *sambhogakaya.*

nirvana (Skt). See *liberation.*

Padmasambhava (Skt; Tib: Guru Rinpoche). The great eighth century Indian tantric master invited to Tibet by King Trisong Detsen to clear away hindrances to the establishment of Buddhism in Tibet.

paramita (Skt). See *six perfections.*

Paramitayana (Skt). The Perfection Vehicle; the first of the two Mahayana paths. This is the gradual path to enlightenment traversed by bodhisattvas practicing the six perfections through the ten bodhisattva levels (*bhumi*) over countless eons of rebirth in samsara for the benefit of all sentient beings. Also called the Sutrayana. See also *Vajrayana.*

Prajnaparamita (Skt). The perfection of wisdom. The *Prajnaparamita* sutras are the teachings of Shakyamuni Buddha in which the wisdom of emptiness and the path of the bodhisattva are set forth. The basis of Nagarjuna's philosophy.

Pratyekabuddhayana (Skt). The Solitary Realizer Vehicle. One of the branches of the *Hinayana.* Practitioners who strive for nirvana in solitude, without relying on a teacher. Cf. *Shravakayana.*

Preliminaries (Tib: ngön-dro). Preliminary practice(s) found in all schools of Tibetan Buddhism, usually done 100,000 times each; the four main ones are recitation of the refuge formula, mandala offerings, prostrations, and Vajrasattva mantra recitation. The Gelug tradition adds five more: guru yoga, water bowl offerings, Damtsig Dorje (Samayavajra) purifying meditation, making *tsa-tsas* (small sacred images, usually made of clay), and the Dorje Khadro (Vajradaka) burnt offering *(jin-sek).*

pride. A deluded mind that holds an inflated or superior image of one-self, preventing spiritual attainment and causing one to disrespect and look down upon others; one of the six principal delusions. *Divine pride* is completely different.

prostration. In Buddhism, the practice of bowing down in respect before one's teacher, a holy object or an altar; there are many different ways of making prostrations.

puja (Skt). Literally, offering; usually used to describe an offering cer-emony such as the *Offering to the Spiritual Master (Guru Puja).*

purification. The eradication from the mind of negative imprints left by past non-virtuous actions, which would otherwise ripen into suffering. The most effective methods of purification employ the four opponent powers of reliance, regret, resolution and the application of antidotes.

refuge. The door to the Dharma path. A Buddhist takes refuge in the Three Jewels fearing the sufferings of samsara and having faith that Bud-dha, Dharma and Sangha have the power to lead him or her out of suf-fering to happiness, liberation or enlightenment.

reincarnation. Rebirth, generally within cyclic existence; one body dies and according to karma, the consciousness goes on to the next life, via the *bardo,* or intermediate state, body.

renunciation (Tib: nge-jung). A heartfelt feeling of complete disgust with cyclic existence such that day and night one yearns for liberation and engages in the practices that secure it. The first of the three principal aspects of the path to enlightenment. Cf. *bodhicitta* and *emptiness.*

Rinpoche (Tib). Literally, "precious one." Generally, a title given to a lama who has intentionally taken rebirth in a human body to continue helping others.

rupakaya (Skt). The "buddha body of form" of a fully enlightened being; the result of the complete and perfect accumulation of merit. It has two aspects—*sambhogakaya,* or "buddha-body of perfect resource," in which the enlightened mind appears to benefit highly realized bodhisattvas, and *nir-*

manakaya, or "buddha-body of perfect emanation," in which the enlightened mind appears to benefit ordinary beings. See also *dharmakaya*.

sadhana (Skt). Method of accomplishment; the step-by-step instructions for practicing the meditations related to a particular meditational deity.

samsara (Skt). See *cyclic existence*.

Sangha (Skt). Spiritual community; the third of the Three Jewels of Refuge. Absolute Sangha are those who have directly realized emptiness; relative Sangha are ordained monks and nuns.

sentient being (Tib: sem-chen). Any unenlightened being; any being whose mind is not completely free from gross and subtle ignorance.

Shakyamuni Buddha (563–483 BC). Fourth of the one thousand founding buddhas of this present world age. Born Siddhartha Gotama, a prince of the Shakya clan in north India, he taught the sutra and tantra paths to liberation and enlightenment; founder of what came to be known as Buddhism. (From the *Skt: buddha*—"fully awake.")

Shantideva. Eighth century Indian Buddhist philosopher and bodhisattva who propounded the Madhyamaka Prasangika view. Wrote the quintessential Mahayana text, *A Guide to the Bodhisattva's Way of Life (Bodhicharyavatara)*.

Shravakayana (Skt). The Hearer Vehicle. One of the branches of the Hinayana. Practitioners (hearers, or *shravakas*) strive for nirvana on the basis of listening to teachings from a teacher. Cf. *Pratyekabuddhayana*.

shunyata (Skt). See *emptiness*.

six perfections (Skt: paramita). Charity, morality, patience, enthusiastic perseverance, concentration and wisdom. See also *Paramitayana*.

six realms. See *cyclic existence*.

stupa (Skt). Buddhist reliquary objects ranging in size from huge to a few inches in height representing the enlightened mind.

suffering. The state of being trapped in cyclic existence under the control of delusion and karma; the subject of the first of the four noble truths.

sutra (Skt). A discourse of Shakyamuni Buddha; the pre-tantric division of Buddhist teachings stressing the cultivation of bodhicitta and the practice of the six perfections. See also *Paramitayana*.

Sutrayana (Skt). See *Paramitayana*.

tantra (Skt). Literally, thread, or continuity; the texts of the secret mantra teachings of Buddhism. Often used to refer to these teachings themselves. See also *Vajrayana*. Cf. *sutra*.

Tantrayana (Skt). See *Vajrayana*.

tathagata (Skt; Tib: de-zhin shek- pa). Literally, one who has realized suchness; a buddha.

ten directions. Symbolic way of saying everywhere throughout infinite space: the four cardinal directions, the four intermediate directions, up and down.

thangka (Tib). Tibetan religious painted scroll.

Theravada (Skt). One of the eighteen schools into which the Hinayana split not long after Shakyamuni Buddha's death; the dominant Hinayana school today, prevalent in Thailand, Sri Lanka and Burma, and well represented in the West.

three higher trainings. Morality (ethics), meditation (concentration) and wisdom (insight).

Three Jewels. The object of refuge for a Buddhist: Buddha, Dharma and Sangha.

three principal paths. The three main divisions of the lam-rim: renunciation, bodhicitta and right view.

Three Precious Sublime Ones or *Triple Gem*. See *Three Jewels*.

tsa-tsa (tib). See *preliminaries*.

Tsongkhapa, Lama Je (1357–1417). Founder of the Gelug tradition of Tibetan Buddhism and revitalizer of many sutra and tantra lineages and the monastic tradition in Tibet.

tum-mo. See inner fire.

Tushita (Skt; Tib: Ganden). The pure land of Buddha Maitreya.

Vajrayana (Skt). The adamantine vehicle; the second of the two Maha-yana paths. It is also called Tantrayana or Mantrayana. This is the quickest vehicle of Buddhism as it allows certain practitioners to attain enlighten-ment within one single lifetime of this degenerate age. See also *tantra.*

vinaya (Skt; Tib: dül-wa). The Buddha's teachings on ethical discipline (morality), monastic conduct and so forth; one of the three baskets.

vipashyana. See insight meditation.

wheel of life. Usually refers to a pictorial representation of cyclic existence, whose rim is the twelve links of dependent arising and whose hub shows the three poisons of ignorance, attachment and hatred.

wisdom. Different levels of insight into the nature of reality. There are, for example, the three wisdoms of hearing, contemplation and meditation. Ultimately, there is the wisdom realizing emptiness, which frees beings from cyclic existence and eventually brings them to enlightenment.

Bibliography

Cleary, Thomas (tr.). *The Flower Ornament Scripture: A Translation of the Avatamsaka Sutra.* Boston: Shambhala Publications, 1984, 1993.

Conze, Edward (tr.). *The Perfection of Wisdom in Eight Thousand Lines & Its Verse Summary.* San Francisco: Four Seasons Foundation, 1973, 1990.

Dhargyey, Geshe Ngawang. *The Tibetan Tradition of Mental Development.* Dharamsala, 1974, 1985.

McDonald, Kathleen. *How to Meditate: A Practical Guide.* Boston: Wisdom Publications, 1984, 2005.

Tsongkhapa, Lama Je. *The Great Treatise on the Stages of the Path to Enlightenment, Volumes 1, 2 & 3.* Ithaca, NY: Snow Lion Publications, 2000, 2002, 2004.

Yeshe, Lama Thubten. *Becoming the Compassion Buddha: Tantric Mahamudra for Everyday Life.* Boston: Wisdom Publications, 2003.

———. *Becoming Vajrasattva: The Tantric Path of Purification.* Boston: Wisdom Publications, 1994, 2004.

———. *The Bliss of Inner Fire: Heart Practice of the Six Yogas of Naropa.* Boston: Wisdom Publications, 1998.

———. *Introduction to Tantra: The Transformation of Desire.* Boston: Wisdom Publications, 1987, 2001.

Zopa Rinpoche, Lama Thubten. *Teachings from the Vajrasattva Retreat.* Boston: Lama Yeshe Wisdom Archive, 2000.

The Maitreya Project

K USHINAGAR, IN NORTHERN INDIA, is one of the "Eight Great Places of Buddhist Pilgrimage"—the site of the historical Buddha's passing away. According to Buddhist scripture, in the distant future—during the life of Maitreya Buddha—Kushinagar will again be a powerful place.

Buddha Maitreya will teach the path of loving-kindness, which is the root cause of peace at every level of society. By developing the qualities of loving-kindness within themselves, individuals bring peace to their families, communities and the world. This is the only way to bring about lasting peace, which cannot be legislated or enforced by political means.

At Kushinagar, the Maitreya Project is building a magnificent 152-metre/500-foot-tall bronze statue of Maitreya. The name Maitreya comes from the Sanskrit word for love, *maitri*, and the form of Maitreya is considered to embody loving-kindness.

Buddhists do not worship statues and religious artifacts. The Buddha image is used as an inspiration for creating and spreading positive human qualities—in this case, loving-kindness, peace, compassion and wisdom.

In this way, the Maitreya Buddha statue, like other forms of religious art, is a highly beneficial form of spiritual support—not because of the physical statue itself, but because of the inner feelings of devotion and inspiration that are experienced by the individual in contact with that art.

The Maitreya statue will be an enduring monument, evoking positive change in the hearts and minds of people from all over the world.

The scope of the Maitreya Project is intended to bring as much benefit to as many as possible for as long as possible—spiritually, in education and healthcare, and economically, through the direct and indirect creation of employment opportunities in northern India.

Maitreya Project's social services will include extensive educational programs and healthcare of international standard, serving communities where literacy rates are very low and where the majority of families presently live in poverty and rely on subsistence agriculture and menial labor.

In both the long and short term, the Maitreya Project will contribute significantly to the economy of the region and aims to become a model of socially responsible development—environmentally sustainable and built to last at least 1,000 years.

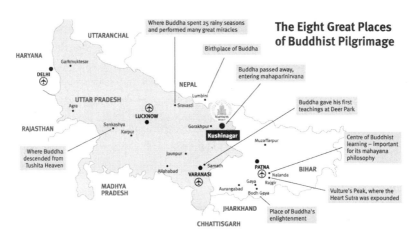

The Eight Great Places of Buddhist Pilgrimage

Where Buddha spent 25 rainy seasons and performed many great miracles

Birthplace of Buddha

Buddha passed away, entering mahaparinirvana

Buddha gave his first teachings at Deer Park

Centre of Buddhist learning – important for its mahayana philosophy

Where Buddha descended from Tushita Heaven

Vulture's Peak, where the Heart Sutra was expounded

Place of Buddha's enlightenment

HARYANA · UTTARANCHAL · DELHI · NEPAL · UTTAR PRADESH · LUCKNOW · RAJASTHAN · Garhmuktesar · Agra · Sankashya · Karpur · Lumbini · Sravasti · Gorakhpur · Kushinagar · Muzaffarpur · Jaunpur · Allahabad · Samath · PATNA · Nalanda · BIHAR · VARANASI · Gaya · Rajgir · Aurangabad · Bodh Gaya · MADHYA PRADESH · JHARKHAND · CHHATTISGARH

The statue will act as a catalyst and sustaining influence for Kushinagar and northern India's development in ways that honor and support the region's rich spiritual heritage.

World focus, inspiration, and Buddhist tradition are the reasons for the size of the Maitreya statue, which continues the ancient tradition of building very large Buddha statues—the more notable a statue is, the more people will hear of it, see it, and have the chance to benefit from it. Loving-kindness—the cause of peace—is more crucial than ever in the world today. The size and scale of the Project are intended to make that statement and to be a constant reminder that real peace is achievable only through loving-kindness, one heart at a time.

The Maitreya Project was the compassionate heart wish of the late Tibetan Buddhist master Lama Yeshe, who devoted his life to making Buddha's teachings available to people worldwide, and who, through his wisdom, warmth, kindness and joy, touched the hearts of thousands of people. Lama's wish is being fulfilled by his heart disciple, Lama Zopa Rinpoche, spiritual director of Maitreya Project and the FPMT.

Please visit www.maitreyaproject.org to learn more about this extraordinary project.

LAMA YESHE WISDOM ARCHIVE

The LAMA YESHE WISDOM ARCHIVE (LYWA) is the collected works of Lama Thubten Yeshe and Lama Thubten Zopa Rinpoche. The ARCHIVE was founded in 1996 by Lama Zopa Rinpoche, its spiritual director, to make available in various ways the teachings it contains. Publication of books of edited teachings for free distribution is one of the ways.

Lama Yeshe and Lama Zopa Rinpoche began teaching at Kopan Monastery, Nepal, in 1970. Since then, their teachings have been recorded and transcribed. At present we have more than 10,000 hours of digital audio and some 60,000 pages of raw transcript on our computers. Many recordings, mostly teachings by Lama Zopa Rinpoche, remain to be transcribed, and as Rinpoche continues to teach, the number of recordings in the ARCHIVE increases accordingly. Most of our transcripts have been neither checked nor edited.

Here at the LYWA we are making every effort to organize the transcription of that which has not yet been transcribed, edit that which has not yet been edited, and generally do the many other tasks detailed below. In all this, we need your financial help. Please contact us for more information:

LAMA YESHE WISDOM ARCHIVE
PO Box 356, Weston, MA 02493, USA
Telephone (781) 259-4466; Fax (678) 868-4806
info@LamaYeshe.com
www.LamaYeshe.com

THE ARCHIVE TRUST

The work of the LAMA YESHE WISDOM ARCHIVE falls into two categories: archiving and dissemination.

Archiving requires managing the recordings of teachings by Lama Yeshe and Lama Zopa Rinpoche that have already been collected, collecting recordings of teachings given but not yet sent to the ARCHIVE, and collecting recordings of Lama Zopa's on-going teachings, talks, advice and so forth as he travels the world for the benefit of all. Incoming media are then catalogued and stored safely while being kept accessible for further work.

We organize the transcription of audio, add the transcripts to the already existent database of teachings, manage this database, have transcripts checked, and make transcripts available to editors or others doing research on or practicing these teachings.

Other archiving activities include working with video and photographs of the Lamas and digitizing ARCHIVE materials.

Dissemination involves making the Lamas' teachings available through various avenues including books for free distribution, books for sale through Wisdom Publications, lightly edited transcripts, audio CDs, DVDs, articles in *Mandala* and other magazines and on our Web site. Irrespective of the medium we choose, the teachings require a significant amount of work to prepare them for distribution.

This is just a summary of what we do. The ARCHIVE was established with virtually no seed funding and has developed solely through the kindness of many people, some of whom we have mentioned at the front of this book and most of the others on our Web site. We sincerely thank them all.

Our further development similarly depends upon the generosity of those who see the benefit and necessity of this work, and we would be extremely grateful for your help.

The ARCHIVE TRUST has been established to fund the above activities and we hereby appeal to you for your kind support. If you would like to make a contribution to help us with any of the above tasks or to sponsor books for free distribution, please contact us at our Weston address.

The LAMA YESHE WISDOM ARCHIVE is a 501(c)(3) tax-deductible, non-profit corporation dedicated to the welfare of all sentient beings and totally dependent upon your donations for its continued existence.

Thank you so much for your support. You may contribute by mailing a check, bank draft or money order to our Weston address; by making a donation on our secure Web site; by mailing us your credit card number or phoning it in; or by transferring funds directly to our bank—ask us for details.

LAMA YESHE WISDOM ARCHIVE MEMBERSHIP
In order to raise the money we need to employ a fulltime editing team to make available the tens of thousands of pages of unedited transcript mentioned above, we have established a membership plan. Membership costs US$1,000 and its main benefit is that you will be helping make the Lamas' incredible teachings available to a worldwide audience. More direct and tangible benefits to you personally include free Lama Yeshe and Lama Zopa Rinpoche books from the ARCHIVE and Wisdom Publications, a year's subscription to *Mandala*, a year of monthly pujas by the monks and nuns at Kopan Monastery with your personal dedication, and access to an exclusive members-only section of our Web site containing special, unpublished teachings currently unavailable to others. Please see www.LamaYeshe.com for more information.

MONTHLY E-LETTER
Each month we send out a free e-letter containing our latest news and a previously unpublished teaching by Lama Yeshe or Lama Zopa Rinpoche. To see more than fifty back-issues or to subscribe with your email address, please go to our Web site.

The Foundation for the Preservation of the Mahayana Tradition

The Foundation for the Preservation of the Mahayana Tradition (FPMT) is an international organization of Buddhist meditation study and retreat centers, both urban and rural, monasteries, publishing houses, healing centers and other related activities founded in 1975 by Lama Thubten Yeshe and Lama Thubten Zopa Rinpoche. At present, there are more than 145 FPMT activities in over thirty countries worldwide.

The FPMT has been established to facilitate the study and practice of Mahayana Buddhism in general and the Tibetan Gelug tradition, founded in the fifteenth century by the great scholar, yogi and saint, Lama Je Tsong-khapa, in particular.

Every two months, the Foundation publishes a wonderful news journal, *Mandala*, from its International Office in the United States of America. To subscribe or view back issues, please go to the *Mandala* Web site, www.mandalamagazine.org, or contact:

FPMT
1632 SE 11th Avenue, Portland, OR 97214
Telephone (503) 808-1588; Fax (503) 808-1589
info@fpmt.org
www.fpmt.org

The FPMT Web site also offers teachings by His Holiness the Dalai Lama, Lama Yeshe, Lama Zopa Rinpoche and many other highly respected teachers in the tradition, details about the FPMT's educational programs, audio through FPMT radio, a complete listing of FPMT centers all over the world and in your area, and links to FPMT centers on the Web, where you will find details of their programs, and to other interesting Buddhist and Tibetan home pages.

DISCOVERING BUDDHISM AT HOME

*Achieving the limitless potential of your mind,
achieving all peace and happiness*

This fourteen-module program is designed as an experiential course in Tibetan Buddhist philosophy and practice. The teachings contained herein are drawn from the Gelug tradition of Lama Tsongkhapa, a great fourteenth century saint and scholar. These teachings come in an unbroken lineage from Shakyamuni Buddha, who first imparted them some 2,600 years ago, since when they have passed directly from teacher to disciple down to the present day.

The realizations of Shakyamuni Buddha cannot be measured but it is said that the Buddha gained direct insight into the nature of reality, perfected the qualities of wisdom, compassion and power, and then revealed the path to accomplish those same realizations to his disciples. The Buddha's teachings have been presented in various ways by different holy beings over the centuries to make them more accessible to those of us who did not have the opportunity to meet the Buddha himself. Lama Tsongkhapa was one such holy being and his teachings on the *lam-rim* (graduated path to enlightenment) are the heart of the Discovering Buddhism at Home program.

In addition, two contemporary masters, Lama Thubten Yeshe (1935–1984), and Lama Zopa Rinpoche (1945–), have imparted these teachings to their students in a deep and experiential way, leading thousands of seekers to discover for themselves the truth of what the Buddha taught. The methods and teachings found in this program also reflect the unique styles of these two great teachers and are meant to help students get an experiential taste of the Buddha's words.

There are two levels of participation that you may choose from when you embark on this program. Within each of the fourteen modules there are discourses, meditations and other practices, readings and assessment questions. As a casual student you may do some or all of the above as you wish. Alternatively, you can engage in this program as a certificate student, in which case you will see on the summary sheet that comes with each module the requirements to be fulfilled. With each module you also receive a Completion Card, which you have to fill out if you want to get a certificate. Although we recommend doing the modules in order, you don't have to. When you have completed all fourteen cards you can receive the certificate of completion issued by the

Education Department of FPMT and the FPMT's spiritual director, Lama Zopa Rinpoche, which simply gives you the satisfaction of having completed a very comprehensive engagement with the path to enlightenment.

Discovering Buddhism at Home is intended to be more than an academic undertaking and if you want to gain some experience of what the Buddha taught you are encouraged to make it a personal goal to fulfill all of the course requirements and thus qualify for the completion certificate, which symbolizes your commitment to spiritual awakening. When you get it you should rejoice deeply, being moved by how your mind has changed in the process.

The Discovering Buddhism at Home package includes the following:
A different Western teacher teaches each module. You will receive these teachings on audio CD (the length of each module varies but there are approximately 4–8 teaching CDs per module). Additionally, you will receive audio CDs of the guided meditations (2–4 CDs per module).

Each module also has a Course Materials text CD containing all the written transcripts of the teachings and meditations in printed form and a text CD containing the Required Reading materials for all fourteen modules (but not the commercially published books, which you have to acquire on your own and are listed under Required and Suggested Reading).

An on-line bulletin board has been created exclusively for Discovering Buddhism at Home participants. When you purchase your first module you will receive instructions on how to join and thus enhance your learning experience through this virtual discussion group.

Each module costs US$40. If you fulfill all the requirements it should take you about two months to complete each one. However, you are free to buy the modules whenever it suits you; when you finish one you can simply buy the next. If you want to receive a completion certificate you will also receive the support of an FPMT elder, who will reply to your answers to the assessment questions to ensure that your understanding is on track with and to guide you through the fourteen modules. You can purchase the modules directly from the FPMT shop at www.fpmt.org/shop or by emailing materials@fpmt.org.

Other teachings of Lama Yeshe and Lama Zopa Rinpoche currently available

Books published by Wisdom Publications

Wisdom Energy, by Lama Yeshe and Lama Zopa Rinpoche
Introduction to Tantra, by Lama Yeshe
Transforming Problems, by Lama Zopa Rinpoche
The Door to Satisfaction, by Lama Zopa Rinpoche
Becoming Vajrasattva: The Tantric Path of Purification, by Lama Yeshe
The Bliss of Inner Fire, by Lama Yeshe
Becoming the Compassion Buddha, by Lama Yeshe
Ultimate Healing, by Lama Zopa Rinpoche
Dear Lama Zopa, by Lama Zopa Rinpoche
How to Be Happy, by Lama Zopa Rinpoche (forthcoming)

About Lama Yeshe:
Reincarnation: The Boy Lama, by Vicki Mackenzie

About Lama Zopa Rinpoche:
The Lawudo Lama, by Jamyang Wangmo

You can get more information about and order the above titles at www.wis-dompubs.org or call toll free in the USA on 1-800-272-4050.

Transcripts, practices and other materials

See the LYWA and FPMT Web sites for transcripts of teachings by Lama Yeshe and Lama Zopa Rinpoche and other practices written or compiled by Lama Zopa Rinpoche.

DVDs of Lama Zopa Rinpoche

There are many available: see the FPMT Web site for more information.

What to do with Dharma teachings

The Buddhadharma is the true source of happiness for all sentient beings. Books like the one in your hand show you how to put the teachings into practice and integrate them into your life, whereby you get the happiness you seek. Therefore, anything containing Dharma teachings, the names of your teachers or holy images is more precious than other material objects and should be treated with respect. To avoid creating the karma of not meeting the Dharma again in future lives, please do not put books (or other holy objects) on the floor or underneath other stuff, step over or sit upon them, or use them for mundane purposes such as propping up wobbly tables. They should be kept in a clean, high place, separate from worldly writings, and wrapped in cloth when being carried around. These are but a few considerations.

Should you need to get rid of Dharma materials, they should not be thrown in the rubbish but burned in a special way. Briefly: do not incinerate such materials with other trash, but alone, and as they burn, recite the mantra OM AH HUM. As the smoke rises, visualize that it pervades all of space, carrying the essence of the Dharma to all sentient beings in the six samsaric realms, purifying their minds, alleviating their suffering, and bringing them all happiness, up to and including enlightenment. Some people might find this practice a bit unusual, but it is given according to tradition. Thank you very much.

Dedication

Through the merit created by preparing, reading, thinking about and sharing this book with others, may all teachers of the Dharma live long and healthy lives, may the Dharma spread throughout the infinite reaches of space, and may all sentient beings quickly attain enlightenment.

In whichever realm, country, area or place this book may be, may there be no war, drought, famine, disease, injury, disharmony or unhappiness, may there be only great prosperity, may everything needed be easily obtained, and may all be guided by only perfectly qualified Dharma teachers, enjoy the happiness of Dharma, have love and compassion for all sentient beings, and only benefit and never harm each other.

LAMA THUBTEN YESHE was born in Tibet in 1935. At the age of six, he entered the great Sera Monastic University, Lhasa, where he studied until 1959, when the Chinese invasion of Tibet forced him into exile in India. Lama Yeshe continued to study and meditate in India until 1967, when, with his chief disciple, Lama Thubten Zopa Rinpoche, he went to Nepal. Two years later he established Kopan Monastery, near Kathmandu, in order to teach Buddhism to Westerners. In 1974, the Lamas began making annual teaching tours to the West, and as a result of these travels a worldwide network of Buddhist teaching and meditation centers—the Foundation for the Preservation of the Mahayana Tradition (FPMT)— began to develop. In 1984, after an intense decade of imparting a wide variety of incredible teachings and establishing one FPMT activity after another, at the age of forty-nine, Lama Yeshe passed away. He was reborn as Ösel Hita Torres in Spain in 1985 and recognized as the incarnation of Lama Yeshe by His Holiness the Dalai Lama in 1986. Lama's remarkable story is told in Vicki Mackenzie's book, *Reincarnation: The Boy Lama* (Wisdom Publications, 1996) and Adele Hulse's official biography, *Big Love, Lama Yeshe* (forthcoming).

DR. NICHOLAS RIBUSH, MB, BS, is a graduate of Melbourne University Medical School (1964) who first encountered Buddhism at Kopan Monastery, Nepal, in 1972. Since then he has been a student of Lama Yeshe and Lama Zopa Rinpoche and a full time worker for their international organization, the Foundation for the Preservation of the Mahayana Tradition (FPMT). He was a monk from 1974 to 1986. He established FPMT archiving and publishing activities at Kopan in 1973 and with Lama Yeshe founded Wisdom Publications in 1975. Between 1981 and 1996 he served variously as Wisdom's director, editorial director and director of development. Over the years he has edited and published many teachings by His Holiness the Dalai Lama, Lama Yeshe, Lama Zopa Rinpoche and many other teachers and established and/or directed several other FPMT activities, including the International Mahayana Institute, Tushita Mahayana Meditation Centre, the Enlightened Experience Celebration, Mahayana Publications, Kurukulla Center for Tibetan Buddhist Studies and now the LAMA YESHE WISDOM ARCHIVE. He was a member of the FPMT board of directors from its inception in 1983 until 2002.